Strategy *360*

10 Steps to Creating a Complete
Game Plan for Business & Life

Randall Bell

OWNERS MANUAL PRESS
LAGUNA BEACH, CALIFORNIA
OwnersManual.com

OwnersManual.com

LeadershipCouncil.com

Printed in the United States of America

12 11 10 09 08   5 4 3 2 1

ISBN 978-1-933969-16-9

Library of Congress Control Number: 2008903266

Photo credits:
pages 68, 126, 127 top: public domain
All other photos by Randall Bell

Book design and layout by D. & F. Scott Publishing, Inc., N. Richland Hills, Texas

Dedicated to Melanie, Michael, Steven, Britten, and Drake

Contents

Acknowledgments

I would like to thank Neil Balholm, who provided considerable insights throughout the writing of this book; Diane Armitage, who provided initial editing; my brother Jim Bell, who reviewed the manuscript several times; and Bill Scott, who did an outstanding job with copy editing and final layout.

Introduction

Today is fairly typical. So far, I have received two FedEx packages—one assignment involving a flood and the other dealing with a major landslide. I still need to finish looking at the documents that arrived yesterday dealing with widespread contamination in Colorado. A client just called from Hawaii to give an update on the state's largest pesticide spill. Before my business partner left for the airport, we discussed one of our cases involving a deranged woman who went into an office building and started shooting people. Two weeks ago, I was in Pennsylvania with the owner of the land where United Flight 93 crashed on September 11, and my secretary just handed me my itinerary to go to St. Louis next Tuesday to inspect a nuclear waste landfill. On the way out, she added that the nuclear fuel pellet on my bookshelf was making her nervous and made some crack about Homer Simpson.

Figuring out big problems is just a part of my life.

I've been working in the field of damage economics and strategic planning for about two decades. My days are spent working with tough situations that involve many lives and hundreds of millions of dollars. It's my job to sort out the problems, determine the financial losses, and find solutions.

I imagine I'm the only person in the world who has visited the melted-down nuclear reactors at Chernobyl, consulted for the owner of the "Heaven's Gate" mass suicide mansion in Rancho Santa Fe, California, stood at the smoking rubble after the terrorist attack on the World Trade Center, advised the government concerning the nuclear test sites at the Bikini Atoll, spoken to student protestors at Tiananmen Square, driven a Humvee through flooded neighborhoods in New Orleans after hurricane Katrina, and sat at the kitchen table with Nicole Brown Simpson's family.

While most of these situations involved dramatic circumstances, each one has provided amazing lessons. In fact, I feel as if a truck has backed up and dropped a huge load of remarkable experiences on me.

Winston Churchill said,

> *A Pessimist sees the difficulty in every opportunity;*
> *an Optimist sees the opportunity in every difficulty*

Through it all, I've gained some insights—not only on the problems themselves—but on what caused them, how effectively they were managed, how they could have been avoided, and, in some cases, even how to create something worthwhile out of them.

Problems create lessons, and lessons create value. At the very least, these assignments provide an opportunity to study both effective and ineffective strategies, and to develop truly effective game plans for going forward.

The Business of Problem Solving

Most people have no trouble behaving and performing well when everything is coasting along. But a major crisis shocks the system; it exposes the core values embedded in both individuals and organizations. While lots of people want to jump right to "success," the fact is that success is a function of problem solving. The better we get at facing a challenge head on and solving it, the more achievements we will enjoy.

While we all presumably want success, finding the right formula can be elusive. Those who chase after it remind me of five-year-old kids playing soccer. They run around in a swarm, clamoring at their chance to kick that big ball of "success."

They chase the idea that success is a result of "goal setting"—but even the Menendez Brothers had "goals."

The ball gets kicked over to the idea of "positive thinking"—but even in the immediate aftermath of Chernobyl, Soviet leader Mikhail Gorbachev was a "positive thinker," so much so that he felt he could hide a nuclear meltdown from the world.

Then the ball rolls over to the "be proactive" or "just do it" camps. Certainly those concepts have merit, but activity doesn't necessarily equal accomplishment.

The "success gurus" of our day stress honesty. I think honesty is fundamental, but once I got hit up by a panhandler on the Santa Monica Pier who told me he was going to use my money to buy drugs. He believed that his "honest" approach would score a few bucks.

The same success gurus chase after the idea of developing a positive self-image; but research says our prisons are full of people who test out with great self-images. In fact, prison inmates generally have better self-esteem than college students.

So, the pack rushes over to "everybody wins." The "win-win" concept is great most of the time, but do we really want child molesters, terrorists, and drug pushers to "win?"

In today's competitive environment, more and more emphasis is spent in "drilling down" into deeper levels of specialty. I appreciate that, as I'm one of less than ten people in my specific field. But I am also convinced that everyone, no matter how specialized, can benefit by also going the other direction and getting a clear "big picture" of the organizational landscape in front of them.

The Art of Achievement

After studying and working on a number of high-profile cases, I've determined that achieving real success is more involved than what some "success gurus" would have us think. There is no single target. Honesty by itself will not get you to the top. Goals will not do it alone. Knowing the right people and demonstrating "people skills" are just part of the picture. We must combine all of these concepts into our particular specialties.

My core specialty is in the field of real estate damage economics. In other words, I measure the loss of property values resulting from some type of detrimental condition, such as earthquakes, hurricanes, terrorist attacks, environmental contamination, crimes, and so forth. (The details and mechanics of my specialty are the topic of another discussion. If you are interested, read my textbook, *Real Estate Damages*, or my books *Home Owners Manual*, or *Disasters: Wasted Lives, Valuable Lessons*). However, this book is not about real estate or my particular specialty, although I do use many of my experiences to illustrate the key points.

Having worked on dozens of these cases for many years, the scope of my work has evolved beyond economics and into strategic planning. Having been involved with several world-class projects, I have been fortunate to work with many of the top experts in their respective fields from all over the world. Working at this level, there is no time for happy talk or excuses. We must work as a team. We must have a clear game plan. We must produce bottom line results.

Strategic Planning:

The word "strategy" originates from the Greek *statos* meaning "expedition" and *agein* meaning "to lead." Before any journey, there must be a plan, a map, and preparations. Without a strategy, we are prone to just wandering aimlessly. When we possess a strategy, we have studied the situation, have a clear game plan, and are in a position to move forward.

The development of a complete strategic framework—a project I call "Strategy 360"—actually began about twenty years ago as a graduate student at UCLA. Our professor gave us an assignment to write a complete business plan. I began researching and looking for a strategic planning model, that would be (1) comprehensive, (2) straight-forward, and that would (3) integrate completely between organizational and individual objectives. Simply stated, no such framework existed.

After months and months of efforts that included literally hundreds upon hundreds of attempts, I finally came up with the beginnings of a strategic framework that met these criteria.

My work in strategic planning followed into my career, where I continued to refine and improve this framework. As I got called to consult on disaster after disaster, I always took notice of the behaviors and management styles in play before, during, and after the event. I noted that many disasters occurred because of a flawed strategy, or the lack of a plan altogether. On the other hand, I noted that successful organizations and individuals inevitably had a game plan that covered "all the bases."

The Four Most Important Words in "Strategy"

The *Strategy 360* framework centers around four universal concepts; Purpose, People, Productivity, and Progress. Every topic in the world will comfortably fit within one of these four categories. That may seem like oversell, but this model has been tested for years under the most demanding conditions, and it always proves to be effective.

Global Approach

Purpose has its origins in Early French *pose*, which means "question" and Early English *appose* meaning "examine closely" and "interrogate," as well as early French *porpos* meaning "aim," "intention," and "by design." The starting place of any venture is to closely examine, question, and investigate one's core values and mission. To leapfrog over such a step would be as foolish as to set sail without a rudder. Indeed, "Purpose" sets the trajectory in which any person or organization will ultimately travel. "Purpose" includes a combination of "Philosophical" and "Intellectual" issues. It is the values and beliefs of a person or the mission of an organization, coupled with data and knowledge.

People is founded in the Latin *populus*, meaning "population" or a "body of persons" comprising a "community," or a "host of warriors" acting upon character, personal power, influence and the destiny of men. "People" are the ultimate creation and thus they are the ultimate priority. "People" includes both "Sociological" and "Influential" issues.

Productivity is based in the Latin *pro*, meaning "forward" or "in favor of," and *ductus* meaning "to lead." It is a social principle meaning "fit for production" or to "lead or bring forth" and to "create" something strong and of social worth and *valoir* or "value." Without productivity, there is no value. "Productivity" includes a combination of "Environmental," "Financial," and "Physical" issues.

Progress originates from the Latin *progressus*. The roots of this word are *pro* meaning "forward" and *gress* meaning "flow" or "movement," or "moving forward." The "action of walking forward" and the "advancement to higher stages" is taken by the *avant-garde* or "pioneers and innovators." "Progress" includes the categories of "Developmental," "Operational," and "Consequential."

When I need a quick, yet effective game plan, I use the "Purpose," "People," "Productivity," and "Progress" model. For example, if I am in a meeting, I want to listen and understand the purpose of the meeting. (It is surprising how many meetings start out with no clear agenda.) Then I want to know about the people, meaning every person in the meeting, as well as the people that our meeting will impact. Then I want to learn about the current status and level of productivity and finally, I want to know what needs to be done to progress.

In other words, when the meeting is over, there must be a clear sense of "where do we go from here?" I keep this quick strategy in my "back pocket" for use in just about every situation.

Comprehensive Strategic Planning

For more involved projects, I use all ten fundamentals of a complete strategic plan. While I cannot tell anyone how to run their business or life, nor would I want to, I can confidently say that every successful business and person inevitably addresses all of the ten components of a complete strategic plan. If just one element is missing or is out of balance, then the entire entity can get into trouble. It is kind of like a spine, if just one vertebrate goes out of alignment, the entire body shuts down.

Some people and organizations inherently know to address all ten categories. However, many do not, and examining and addressing these ten categories has a remarkable effect. Often they can see what element is missing or out of balance, take some action, and move forward with a complete strategic plan.

Admittedly, the ten categories can be difficult to remember. Accordingly, the "10 Strategies" quickly encapsulate the core element of each of the ten categories. I have made these ten strategies a part of my everyday vocabulary. For example, for the "Philosophical" category, the strategy is "Get the Big Picture." I use this concept at the beginning of every day, with every new assignment, in every business meeting. It stops those who tend to jump prematurely into details, fire drills, and busy work and forces them to take a step back and think about what is important. Likewise, the other nine strategies are useful at getting to what is important on that particular level.

The Global Approach

The four elements of the Global Approach can be expanded into ten fundamental categories within which any topic will ultimately fall.

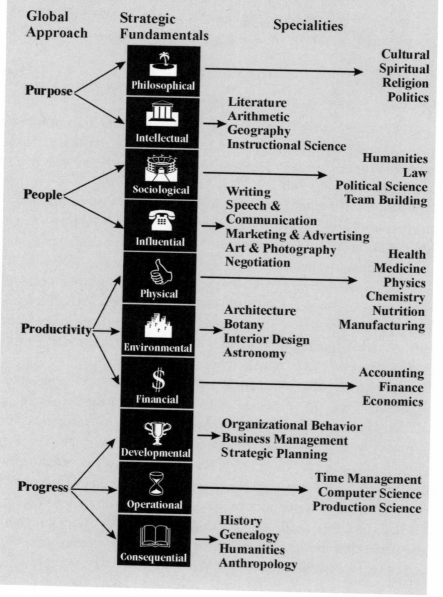

Strategy 360

		Individual Plan	**Organizational Plan**
PURPOSE	**Philosophical**	Ethics Core Values Attitudes & Beliefs	Ethics Mission Statement & Vision Organizational Culture
	Intellectual	Education & Studies Experience & Training	Business Concept Intellectual Property Training & Development
PEOPLE	**Sociological**	Roles Responsibilities Family & Friends	Personnel Strategic Relationships Competitor Analysis
	Influential	Address & Phone Contacts Communication Skills	Target Market PR & Marketing Advertising
PRODUCTIVITY	**Physical**	Health & Fitness Medical Checkups	Products & Services Research & Development
	Environmental	Residence Personal Assets	Facilities Furniture & Equipment Maintenance & Security
	Financial	Personal Finances Budget	Pricing Models Financial Statements Exit Strategies
PROGRESS	**Developmental**	Goals & Development Risk Mitigation	Short & Long Term Goals Expansion Plans Risk Mitigation
	Operational	Key Dates & Calendar Time Management	Systems & Operations Customer Service Crisis Management
	Consequential	Personal Legacy Journal Photos & Mementoes	Organizational Legacy Key Lessons Awards

9

Leadership Model

The Leadership Model illustrates how Left Line (negligent) and Right Line (excessive) behaviors go "out of bounds" and result in failure. On the other hand, navigating within the Bottom Line areas inevitably results in achievement.

		Left Line®	Bottom Line®	Right Line®
PURPOSE	Philosophical	Unprincipled	Adaptive Principled Passionate	Fanatical
	Intellectual	Ignorant	Teachable Knowledgeable Brilliant	Arrogant
PEOPLE	Sociological	Illicit	Lenient Lawful Considerate	Annoying
	Influential	Insensitive	Independent Reliable Supportive	Controlling
PRODUCTIVITY	Physical	Apathetic	Relaxed Fit Competitive	Excessive
	Environmental	Careless	Comfortable Orderly Extraordinary	Harsh
	Financial	Insolvent	Generous Budgeted Wealthy	Greedy
PROGRESS	Developmental	Regressive	Flexible Proactive Determined	Irrational
	Operational	Negligent	Easy-Going Organized Aggresive	Compulsive
	Consequential	Denial	Forgiving Accountable Grateful	Obsessive

As the "Strategy 360" framework evolved, managerial traits and behaviors were integrated into the model in an effort to identify those that were effective and ineffective. This is called the *Strategy 360 Leadership Model*, wherein Left Line (negligent), Right Line (excessive) and Bottom Line (effective) traits are identified. With every disaster or crisis, we can identify those behaviors that caused the problem and those that were effective and ineffective in the aftermath. This model has proven to be very valuable in both identifying the problems and developing strategies for going forward.

Now that you understand the underlying principles and framework of *Strategy 360*, as well as some of its applications, each chapter goes into greater detail with each of the ten categories. Each chapter also introduces one of the "10 Strategies" and identifies several examples of *Left Line*, *Right Line,* and *Bottom Line* behaviors.

As I study and work with some of the most extreme situations around the world, this is the framework I use to analyze the situation. I have also used the *Strategy 360* framework to develop business plans that have resulted in successful multi-million dollar ventures. From speeches at business conventions, to lectures to college or high school students, this framework works in every context. It is simple, complete and effective with both organizations and individuals.

> In my career, where I work with many of the world's most extreme problems and disasters, the five most common words I hear in the aftermath of a tragedy are "We didn't think of that." The "Strategy 360" framework is designed so that we think of every angle of a complete strategic plan.

Any business, career, individual, or household can fill in the *Strategy 360* framework in the way they want. But simply having such a framework ensures that "all the bases" are covered and that a complete strategic plan is in place. This creates value, and ultimately leads to achievement.

Part I

Purpose

Purpose has its origins in Early French *pose*, which means "question" and Early English *appose* meaning "examine closely" and "interrogate," as well as early French *porpos* meaning "aim," "intention," and "by design."

Chapter One

Philosophical

Get the Big Picture

To achieve anything, we must have a strategy. When I walk into a boardroom in New York City to consult on the World Trade Center site, drive the devastated streets of New Orleans after Hurricane Katrina, or cut through the jungle of the Bikini Atoll nuclear weapons test sites, I have a clear strategic plan in place. I have to. Billions of dollars are riding on those decisions.

"The 10 Strategies" are those actually implemented with events that everyone has read about in the newspaper or has seen on television. They not only work with major world events, but with everyday life. They work with clients, business partners, staff, family, and friends. They work at the office, home, school, church, and even on vacation. Simply stated, those who have a clear strategic plan will always get more out of business and life.

The first strategy is to "Get the Big Picture." This is really a philosophical issue that prompts us to look at the complete scene and decide what is important to us, what is not, and where we want to go.

Our bottom line results are ultimately the consequence of our mindset. A noble mindset and a clear purpose will send us on an upward trajectory and ultimately lead to high achievement, while an undisciplined mindset and an unclear purpose will ultimately yield to the powers of gravity and result in chaos and failure. Our purpose, good, bad, or indifferent, sends us in the direction we will go.

A person with "purpose" does not necessarily correlate with their "position." While many who have achieved high positions got there as a result of a clear purpose, some people who have achieved high positions actually remained unsatisfied. This is nearly always a result of a lack of purpose. On the other hand, a clear purpose is what drives one to an upward path and draws others in. A person or organization with a clear agenda, based upon sound core values and principles, will grow and flourish. They know why they are there and what needs to be done. Ridicule is more easily dismissed. They know where they are going.

A sense of purpose and a solid philosophy is available to everyone and every organization, regardless of their history or background. A person can come from a rich, poor, or middle-class background, and may be educated or uneducated. In fact, after all my observations, I am convinced that *intelligence is not measured by IQ; it is a way of thinking*. A sense of purpose, coupled with clarity and core values, is a powerful mix that ignites passion and results in a deeply satisfying path. This concept has value for business management, real estate management, crisis management, and even household management.

This does not mean that a person with a clear purpose and core values will not stumble along the way. Setbacks are inevitable. But people traveling with strong core values know that problems are just opportunities in disguise and see setbacks as valuable lessons on achieving even more. While sure of their mission, they are always open to learning more and improving on the past.

Albert Einstein once said, "The significant problems we face cannot be solved at the same level of thinking we were at when we created them."

If we are truly interested in achievement, we must pause once in a while, examine past setbacks, look at what worked and what didn't, and be willing to adopt—and act on—a more effective mindset.

	Left Line	Bottom Line	Right Line
🌴 **Philosophical**	**Unprincipled**	**Adaptive Principled Passionate**	**Fanatical**

Disaster Is Often the Product of an *Unprincipled* Mindset

Our mindset determines our results. Before any action, there is always a moment when the mind makes a decision. That moment determines if the action is going to go out of bounds or stay within the bottom line of success. The bulk of philosophy serves to shape and determine that quick, but all-important moment when a decision is made. Understanding this helps us understand the roots of a problem, which is a key element of problem solving.

Let me illustrate this point with a case that falls far from an effective mindset—Chernobyl. This was a disaster so enormous that one journalist called it, "the beginning of the end of the world."

To most people, Chernobyl was a monumental environmental disaster, and indeed it was; however, like many disasters, it was *fundamentally* a philosophical failure, resulting from the unprincipled thinking that put the disaster into motion.

Ironically, Chernobyl was caused by a group of scientists who were conducting a safety experiment. They had no plan and no authorization. Essentially, they were curious to see if there was enough electricity stored in a spinning turbine to shut down the reactor. On April 26, 1986, they turned off all seven safety systems and then cut the power to the turbine. They *then* tried to shut down the reactor.

They got their answer.

The nuclear core overheated, and, in their frantic response, the reactor exploded. A full-scale nuclear meltdown began.

If only one of the seven safety measures had been in place, the accident would never have occurred. The blast killed several workers, but far more damage was caused when the nuclear fuel caught on fire.

Visually, a nuclear meltdown looks like little more than a small fire; however, inhaling the smoke shuts the body's central nervous system down in less than ten minutes. As emergency workers responded, many teachers took their students outside to observe the brave firefighters, not knowing that they were actually contributing to the injury or death of their students.

The offender—Reactor 4—was quickly enclosed in a concrete, ten story sarcophagus; and, to this day, it sits next to Reactor 3, which is still in operation. That's right, most people assume that Chernobyl is shut down completely. In fact, only this one reactor is not operational. The concrete sarcophagus is top heavy and has inadequate bracing. It is expected to collapse at some point in the future. If it falls toward Reactor 3, there could easily be another meltdown during our lifetimes.

A Ghost Town under a Blanket of Radioactive Dust

Today, the Chernobyl seventeen-mile radius "exclusion zone" consists of deserted villages, bulldozed towns and the city of Pripyat. When there, my guide and I were the only people in the entire city.

My first impression upon arriving at Chernobyl was that it is an enormous complex of massive buildings. We drove by the two reactors that had been under construction at the time of the disaster. The deserted crane still sat there. We continued past the three operating nuclear generators and then to Reactor 4, the site of the disaster itself. It was strange standing there, alone, next to a six-story gray structure that encloses the greatest nuclear disaster in history.

My guide said that it was safe to go into the damaged reactor for ten minutes. I said, "no thanks." The idea of walking inside the Chernobyl reactor just seemed nuts.

The accident occurred about a week before May Day, a major holiday in Eastern Europe. Deserted rides, such as Ferris wheels and bumper cars, still stood eerily silent. Radioactive dust was everywhere; no matter where we traveled, the Geiger counter stuttered continuous fast clicks. We were being monitored constantly for radio-

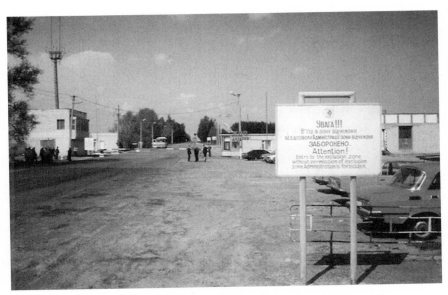

This checkpoint keeps outsiders out of the seventeen-mile
"Chernobyl Exclusion Zone."

This ten-story sarcophagus encloses the world's worst nuclear disaster. It is
supposed to be airtight; however, I saw birds fly in and out of it.

The accident occurred just before May Day as these attractions were being set up. They were deserted like everything else.

The city of Pripyat sits just across the river from Chernobyl. My guide and I were the only people in the entire city.

The Chernobyl Elementary School

This deserted Chernobyl classroom is covered with radioactive fallout.

activity, yet our radioactive exposure still climbed to three to four times the maximum safely allowed.

We deviated from the standard road trip and hiked into overgrown areas to enter a deserted elementary school. The sight was something I'll never forget. Gray, radioactive dust covered everything—from the colorful cartoon murals to the pianos, desks, toys, and dolls in their cribs. In one building, I came across a poster that instructed the children on what to do when the Americans bombed Russia. Ironically, it was covered with radioactive fallout from their own backyard.

The children's names were still posted on a bulletin board for that day's assignments. I stepped over a pair of white shoes that looked just like a pair my own daughter had back home.

In this setting, it didn't take a lot of imagination to envision the children affected by the tragedy. Based on false assurances from their leaders that all was safe, the children inhaled highly radioactive dust, smoke, and fumes. Many died, while others had to have their thyroids removed, resulting in a long scar on their necks called a "nuclear necklace."

This cartoon poster tells the Chernobyl children what to do when the Americans bomb their city. Ironically, it is covered with radioactive dust from their own backyard.

Months later, after visiting the site, I attended a conference where Mikhail Gorbachev disclosed that Chernobyl caused $16 billion in damage. My calculations show that they are not finished counting.

No matter what they thought, they couldn't successfully operate "above the rules"

In their cavalier and arrogant thinking, the Chernobyl scientists didn't stop to think about what they were doing. This is classic Left Line negligence. They saw the rules and regulations as something that didn't apply to them. They viewed these regulations as hurdles, stop signs, and traffic lights that hindered their ability to fly down the road freely. But they failed to realize that, while stop signs and traffic lights may seem a nuisance to us all, we arrive at our destinations more quickly (and alive) when we respect them.

We see similar philosophical issues with the NASA disasters. The space shuttle Challenger blew up soon after takeoff in 1986, and the space shuttle Columbia disintegrated on reentry in 2003. Over the previous thirty-three years, NASA had become one of the most admired organizations in the world, but somewhere it got off track.

The Columbia Accident Investigation Board released a 248-page report that included twenty-nine recommendations, ranging from better camera views of the launch site to handling waste paper near the shuttle. However, the larger question dealt with NASA's management styles and organizational culture. "Broken safety culture" is a term frequently used to describe an organization with outdated procedures, a lack of openness between engineers and managers, and poor coordination. For example, rather than maintaining a safe environment where comments and feedback were OK even if the news was bad, NASA had developed an atmosphere where employees were fearful of bringing up bad news that could delay or stop a mission. Indeed, such messengers, rather than being commended for averting a crisis, could have their careers derailed or be transferred off the project.

Also disturbing was a culture where management would operate outside of its own rules while the engineers were constrained by bureaucratic procedures. Although there were many warning signs regarding damaged tiles on the Columbia and deteriorating O-rings on the Challenger's booster rockets, the NASA management ignored the warning signs in order to achieve mission goals.

In our hypercompetitive world, there is a strong enticement to just leapfrog over philosophical issues and dive directly toward the goal at any cost. Indeed, many Left Line thinkers believe that they are above the philosophical concepts of integrity, honesty, beliefs and values. *An unprincipled mindset is at the core of many—if not most—of the problems I study.*

In the long run, philosophical values cannot be successfully circumvented. To establish long-term success within a company, family, or any organization, one *must* have a supportive and balanced framework in place.

Chernobyl started off with some guys at work one day who thought the rules didn't apply to them. Those scientists are spending the rest of their lives in Russian labor camps. The first lesson from disasters is that *Our mindset determines our results.*

There Is More than One Way to Go Out of Bounds

Chernobyl allows us to address yet another Left Line concept on the Global Matrix, and that is "denial." In the aftermath of Chernobyl, the Soviet leaders denied to the world that there was any problem. How the USSR actually thought it could keep the lid on a full-scale nuclear meltdown is beyond comprehension. Had they simply acknowledged the problem, they could have at least evacuated the people and saved hundreds of lives.

The same philosophical problems apparent at Chernobyl are also commonly seen in other places. Companies illegally dump their wastes to save a buck, yet I work daily to compute environmental liabilities that routinely amount to tens, even hundreds of millions of dollars.

In personal lives, broken rules of drinking and driving lead to misery. In business, broken rules of fiscal imprudence lead to ruin. No matter what the situation, discipline and self-examination are indispensable elements in creating value and balance.

In truth, I, too, had to examine my own thinking when I heard that "a man's true character is revealed as he untangles the Christmas tree lights." This hit me like a ton of bricks because—prior to hearing this—I grumbled and complained every year when my wife asked me to put up the Christmas decorations. My poor attitude certainly distracted from the Christmas cheer in our home as I struggled with those blasted lights!

Whether it's dealing with a nuclear disaster or the annual untangling of one's Christmas tree lights, *the mindset is the starting place*.

The balanced mindset sees—in clear focus—all of the costs and benefits, pleasure and pain, or pros and cons. Achievers see the long-term impact of their decisions just as clearly as they see the immediate benefits.

To illustrate this concept, let's examine the "Focus Factor," which sets up costs and benefits against immediate and long-term outcomes.

With Chernobyl, the leaders saw only the *immediate benefit* of denial—for a brief moment, they tried to appear as if they had everything under control.

Instead, had they possessed a clear and balanced focus, they would have easily recognized the real costs and benefits and admitted their problem. They would have saved children's lives, limited property damage and preserved some level of credibility. No matter how painful an admission, society actually admires and jumps to the aid of the person who admits a mistake *before* being "caught."

Core Values Are the Universal Starting Point

Once, I had the opportunity to speak before a group of pharmaceutical sales people. I told them about Chernobyl and the importance of being grounded philosophically. At the end of the lecture, one person complained that I did not speak enough about "sales strategy."

Two weeks later, I was told that this top sales person had been fired because she had been caught making dummy sales calls and dumping pharmaceutical drug samples in a dumpster, which is a federal offense. In her eagerness to achieve, she jumped over the basic core values,

Focus Factor™

At Chernobyl, the government made the same mistake that many others do. They denied a problem and got the "immediate benefit" of appearing OK. Had they seen all of their options in balance, they would have known that this short-lived "benefit" was outweighed by all of the long-term costs.

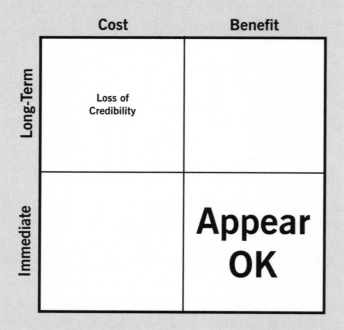

FOCUS FACTOR™
Out of Balance

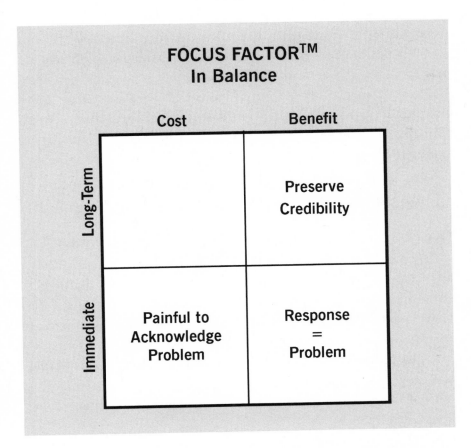

wandered over the Left Line and did something that not only ruined her sales career, but also got her into legal trouble. *No matter what a person's career is, the starting point begins with examining one's core values.*

Fanatics Take a Good Thing Too Far

Mark Twain tells about a church sermon he heard. It was so inspiring that he wanted to put all of his money in the collection plate. But the preacher just kept on going, pounding away at his pulpit, and eventually Mark Twain felt like putting *some* of his money in the plate. As the sermon continued, he decided to not put any money in the plate. By the time the preacher finished, Twain took some money out of the plate!

While a good philosophical mindset is essential, too much of a good thing can be damaging. *Going overboard on the Right Line of fanaticism is just as dangerous as being a Left Line, unprincipled thinker*. Harsh, inflexible, and excessive mindsets are simply out of balance.

Fanatics exist in businesses, families, religions, clubs, neighborhoods, and politics in the form of individuals who are compelled to push their ideas onto others. While offering suggestions, ideas, thoughts, or beliefs to others can be a thoughtful gesture, the person on the receiving end should have the right to say no or disagree.

The passionate person will pursue his objectives, while respecting the rights of others. The fanatic will pursue his objectives at any cost.

Over Regulating Is Similar to Over Medicating a Patient

In my consulting practice, I was once asked by the new CEO of a large firm to assist in diagnosing some serious problems and recommend new, stricter policies to "straighten things out." Upon interviewing and listening to people throughout the company, it became clear to me that stricter policies were not the answer.

The company was already "over medicated" with reams of rules and programs. It got to be so ridiculous that upper management was not only disregarded, but many middle managers were openly rebellious toward them.

My recommendation was to set a new, looser tone in the company.

My client met my recommendation with some skepticism; but deep down he knew that management had gone overboard. I assured him that as a new leader, he had the perfect opportunity to acknowledge the issue and set a tone of accountability without more harsh rules. Together, we developed the outline for a set of new, simpler policies.

During a company meeting, the CEO took several binders of old, obsolete, overbearing policies and ceremoniously dumped them into the trash. He was met by thunderous applause from the employees. Rather than smothering them with another layer of new rules, we facilitated a two-day session where all the employees had input and authorship in developing new standards.

The result yielded only one small binder, but it contained a course of direction that everyone respected. More importantly, the tone was set for accountability without excessive policing. The firm's profits have since soared.

Is Your Brand of "Motivation" Helping Your Bottom Line?

Motivation has a critical role to play with our philosophical mindset. Yet, even motivational efforts can err on the Right Line of fanaticism. I have listened to some motivational speakers and preachers whip a group into a fanatical frenzy. I wonder, though, how many people really retain that motivation once they walk out and get into their cars.

I place motivational speakers into two groups. Those in the first group are basically in the business of selling motivation itself. They have never really accomplished much except for building their motivational seminar companies. These are the ones who tend to err on the Right Line of fanaticism.

The second kind of motivational speakers have genuinely done something great. They have won championships, gold medals, battles, reached the top of their professions, invented something great, built a major company, or accomplished some other immense achievement. These speakers may not stir up frenzied levels of emotion, but their lessons are more valuable as they speak from the position of actually having accomplished something big. In other words, they teach by example.

Sure, they are passionate and competitive, but they also are more grounded and balanced. It can be fascinating to hear about their journeys as they take us through their mindset and speak about the real experiences that got them to where they are. This is real Bottom Line success.

A Balanced Mindset Includes Being *Adaptive*

It is not the biggest or strongest who survive, but those who are adaptable to change. We must be adaptable to survive. If we accept that there is something we can change today that will make our life worse, we must also accept that there is something we can change today to make life or business better. We have the choice every day to do nothing, to make life better or to make life worse. These decisions are driven by a flexible mindset.

The "Zone of Balance™"

Philosophically, a person or organization performs best within the "Zone of Balance." This includes the "Adaptive," "Principled," and "Passionate" areas.

They will inevitably encounter problems in either the "Unprincipled" or "Fanatical" areas.

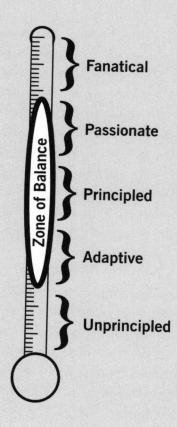

"Achievement" vs. "Success"

Success is actually a trend, rather than a specific event. As the chart illustrates, everyone will have achievements and setbacks, but the real measure of success is the trend over time.

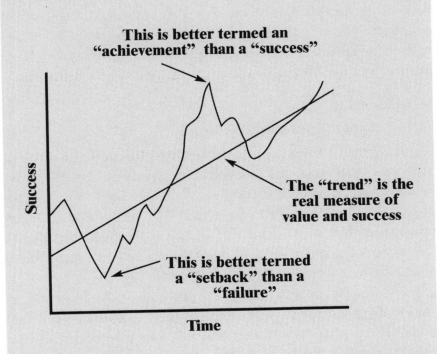

This is better termed an "achievement" than a "success"

The "trend" is the real measure of value and success

This is better termed a "setback" than a "failure"

Success

Time

Lives committed to positive change have meaning, while tentative, unprincipled, and cynical lives tend to offer little value.

The great achievers rarely use the term "failure." It is not a part of their mindset. They prefer the term "setback." They are not always stuck in an overly aggressive mode, but they naturally perform within the entire Bottom Line area. They are aggressive when they need to be, and they back off when appropriate.

The terms *success* and *failure* imply a final point of destination. My observations show that the final arrival of a person or organization is a myth, because there is always more to accomplish. Setbacks are inevitable. Many wise and great people were once insolent and foolish, but they learned from it.

Achievers reserve the right to make mistakes. Mistakes and setbacks do not necessarily break a person; they just reveal the core of that individual's values. An achiever knows to take responsibility for any outcome because excuses are fatal to achievement. *Achievement is not measured by a single act. Achievement is measured by the trend over time.*

McDonald's vs. Luby's
The Value of a *Principled* Philosophy

In October 1984, a man walked into a McDonald's Restaurant in San Ysidro, California, and shot and killed twenty-one people before he was killed by police. McDonald's donated the site to the city and, one night at 10:00 pm, McDonald's bulldozed the building. The next morning, nothing was left but dirt and two palm trees. McDonald's then acquired another site just down the street and constructed a new restaurant, which still stands to this day.

With the McDonald's tragedy, the management made an error in philosophical judgment: bulldozing the crime scene does not fool anybody. In fact, the new McDonald's restaurant is so close to the old site that many people think it is the original location. As the old saying goes, "Denial is not a river in Egypt." Running away from the problem did not solve the problem or fool anybody.

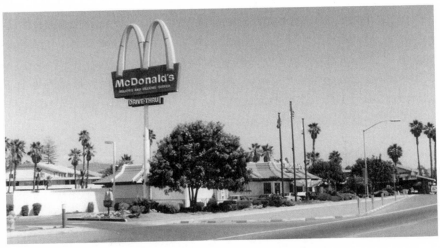

McDonald's built a new restaurant
right down the street from the crime scene site.

At the time, McDonald's was the site of the worst mass murder in national history, until a more heinous crime was committed. In October of 1991, a man drove his truck through the window of a cafeteria-style restaurant called Luby's, which sat on Highway 190 in Killeen, Texas. He shot and killed twenty-three innocent people by walking slowly and calmly through the restaurant, talking nicely to some people and shooting others. Eventually, he turned the gun on himself.

Needless to say, the community and the country were stunned. But the situation was handled differently: Within hours—without any detours to a Madison Avenue public relation firm—company CEO Pete Abeno flew to the site and immediately offered $100,000 to assist the victims and their families. He directly faced the incident and went there to help. All the employees were given a paid leave of absence. Psychologists were retained to help with the emotional damage.

The Luby's sign stayed up, and the restaurant remained intact. The manager told me, "It may sound corny, but our entire attitude was to treat everyone impacted by the tragedy as if they were members of our own family." To me, his comment was not corny at all; in fact, it demonstrated a principled corporate philosophy that existed in this organization long before this tragedy occurred. The company philosophy was not hastily invented or faked when a crisis struck.

As a result of Luby's management style, and in spite of the tragedy, the city of Killeen petitioned Luby's to not abandon the site but, rather, to reopen the facility. The restaurant management extensively remodeled the property and reopened the restaurant about five months later. The restaurant went on to enjoy business as usual.

Luby's demonstrated a winning strategy.

One Does Not Wander Aimlessly into Success

The ultimate goal is not to become a "success" but rather, as Albert Einstein says, a "person of value." Becoming a person of value requires a conscientious effort.

The laws of physics dictate that everything will turn to chaos if not actively acted upon. One does not take a sailing boat out, set course, and expect to reach the destination without continuous effort. Immediately, the winds and tides will shift, turning and throwing the boat off course.

The hurdles never stop, no matter what the state of one's life is:

Prior to September 11, Luby's was the site of the
nation's worst mass-murder.

A memorial sits on the McDonald's mass-murder site.

- If I am not actively exercising, then my fitness is declining.
- If I am not actively earning, expenses will erode my finances.
- If I am not maintaining my friendships and relationships, then they are dissolving.

If progress is not being sought in any particular area, the invariable "winds and tides" will push away achievement. *There must be a deliberate effort.*

Passion Pays Big Dividends

At one time, scientists and doctors said it was anatomically impossible for a human being to run a mile in less than four minutes. Then, an optimist by the name of Roger Banister came along and did it. A lot of people know this, but what is less known is that the four-minute mile was broken again just a few weeks later, and then again and again.

The record had to be broken philosophically first, and then it was broken physically by scores of people.

Some people have such amazing passion that they are a remarkable source of inspiration:

- More than four hundred banks and investors rejected Walt Disney's theme park idea, but he kept going.
- I have a Michael Jordan autographed basketball on my home-office shelf. When my kids complain about some setback, I point at that ball and remind them that Jordan was cut from his high school basketball team. Obviously, he didn't let that setback get in his way.
- I also have a baseball signed by Babe Ruth. Most people know that he set a home run world record, but that great Yankee also set strikeout records as well. On top of that, Babe Ruth was not an orphan as often thought. It was worse than that. His mother and father, while both alive and together, placed him into an orphanage. Yet, he overcame all of that.
- Scientists told Carl Lewis that it was physically impossible for a human to jump more than thirty feet.
- Oprah Winfrey was born to an unwed, fourteen-year-old mother.

Each of these people kept persisting. There must be some risk, some fire and some passion. The one who goes farthest is the one who is willing to take a risk.

Helen Keller said, "Security is mostly a superstition. Life is either a daring adventure or it is nothing."

One can never become what they want to become by remaining where they are.

However Defined, Faith Has an Essential Role

World religions vary, yet they all seem to agree on some significant points. Lives without "soul" ultimately lead nowhere. Faith is the greatest hope-builder of all. People who have faith and who are true to their faith are the better for it.

I once had lunch with a well-known celebrity. We had some common interests, so we exchanged e-mail addresses to correspond. His e-mail address reflected a message that he did not believe in God. I told him that I did. Apparently, there was a significant gap in our ways of thinking.

Through our correspondence, he went on to tell me he did not believe in anything that could not be scientifically proven and added, "If something requires faith, you can count me out."

I told him that atheism is an interesting theory, but it is only a theory that hardly rises to any measure of "fact." Indeed, the very science in which he has so much confidence has a rule that "one cannot prove a negative." In other words, one cannot "scientifically prove" that no God exists, until one searches the universe and verifies that no God exists anywhere. He was annoyed with my observation that, like it or not, by embracing atheism he was putting his faith in an unproven theory. The point is, no matter how one defines their personal philosophies, faith in *something* is required. *Faith is an inevitable aspect of life. We are merely faced with a choice of where to put it.*

Mission Statements

All successful people and organization have a clear purpose. Ask yourself, "What sets me and my organization apart from the rest? What special abilities do we offer that nobody else has? Why are these valuable? Who benefits from our unique abilities?"

No matter what our philosophical positions may be, mission statements are one of the most effective means of really contemplating and defining who we are and what we stand for. An effective mission statement defines a direction and provides a focus. Mission statements apply not only to businesses and corporations, but are also valid for families, teams, and individuals. There are really no rules. They can be long or short, but they should clearly state what is important to you and your objectives. A mission statement that is imposed on others is not as useful as one that has authorship by those who are expected to follow it. It can be stuck on a refrigerator, a bathroom mirror, or a calendar where it can be reviewed often. The important thing is that, although they are written down *now*, they can always be updated later.

Philosophical Insights

- We are what we value.
- True character is revealed when a problem arises.
- Many disasters and successes actually have their roots in the philosophical strengths or weaknesses of the individuals within the organization.
- Too often, people skip over defining their core values and go straight to their goals and tasks. This is a mistake.
- Denial and blame are effective ways of making a small problem a big one.
- There is no "neutral." As soon as a ship sets sail, the tides and winds will blow it off course without action.
- You will become what you constantly think about.
- Be unreasonable of what you expect of yourself.
- How important you think you are sets the standards that you will achieve.
- You can't steal second base with your foot stuck on first.
- Work you love is better than play . . . any day of the week!
- Faith is inevitable. It is only a question of where you put it.
- It is a myth that mission statements are only for corporations. They are also for teams, families, and individuals.
- Write a mission statement that defines your objectives and philosophy
- Write down a mission statement now. It can always be updated later.

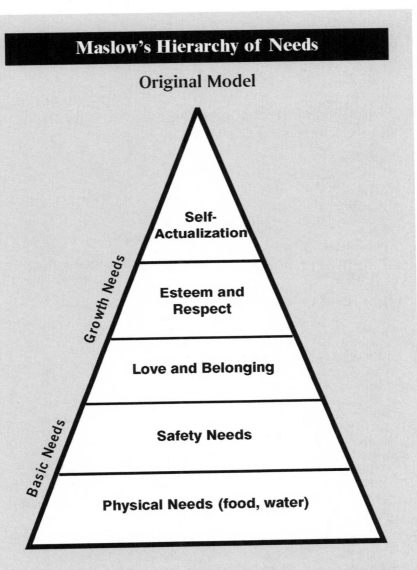

Created by Abraham Maslow, "Maslow's Hierarchy of Needs" illustrates the hierarchy of human needs. As the basic needs are satisfied, higher needs come into play. The ultimate need, "Self-Actualization," is the process of determining what one's ultimate role in life is and then filling that role.

Mission Statements

Following is a list of balanced philosophical values that can assist in formulating an effective business plan.

Affectionate	Disciplined	Intelligent	Reverent
Aggressive	Dominate	Just	Responsible
Amicable	Empathetic	Kind	Secure
Attentive	Empowered	Knowledgeable	Self-confident
Authoritative	Encouraging	Listener	Self-controlled
Balanced	Energetic	Leader	Self-motivated
Benevolent	Enthusiastic	Lively	Self-sufficient
Bold	Ethical	Loving	Sensitive
Broadminded	Excellent	Loyal	Service-
Brave	Entrepreneurial	Mannered	Oriented
Caring	Extra-miler	Moderate	Sincere
Cautious	Fair	Modest	Sober
Charitable	Faithful	Motivated	Social
Chaste	Family Focused	Open-minded	Solvent
Cheerful	Focused	Optimistic	Spiritual
Civil	Forgiving	Obedient	Steadfast
Clean	Fit	Open	Supportive
Committed	Friendly	Organized	Tactful
Communicative	Frugal	Passionate	Teachable
Competent	Generous	Persistent	Team player
Confident	Gentle	Personable	Temperate
Considerate	Goal-oriented	Physically Fit	Thoughtful
Consistent	Grateful	Polite	Thought leader
Convictions	Harmonious	Positive	Thrifty
Coolheaded	Healthy Ego	Prepared	Tolerant
Cooperative	Helpful	Pride	Tranquil
Courageous	Honest	Productive	Truthful
Creative	Hopeful	Prudent	Trustworthy
Decent	Hospitable	Punctual	Valuable
Decisive	Humble	Quality-	Visionary
Dependable	Humorous	oriented	Warm
Determined	Industrious	Reasonable	Worthy
Devoted	Innovative	Reliable	Wise
Dignified	Insightful	Resilient	
Diligent	Integrity	Resourceful	

Chapter Two

Intellectual
Do the Homework

"Get the Big Picture," from the last chapter, is a philosophical matter aimed at compelling ourselves to decide what is really important. What constitutes the "big picture" is a compilation of our values, beliefs, preferences, thoughts, and feelings.

Our complete "purpose" is composed of *both* "big picture" philosophies and feelings, as well as information gained from "doing our homework." Indeed, many poor choices have been made where one "felt really good" about their decision, but failed to yield to common sense or gathering any information.

Information is "king," and we get that data by rolling up our sleeves, digging in and really studying the issues. Losers and drifters usually think they know everything, so that attitude puts them out of the game from the start. Conventional information, such as from schools and universities will get conventional results. Of course, that information is essential, but every real player has it. Getting proprietary data puts a team at a distinct advantage. Training and development is a continual requirement. We must constantly monitor the market and dig in for insights that others don't know about or are too lazy to get. It takes good old tenacious homework, but it is worth it. Digging out superior information brings superior results.

Intelligence is not so much a natural aptitude as it is one's will and capacity to research and discover their needs, gather information, study the alternatives, build experience, and then raise the standards and teach others.

During the school years and early careers, one actively strives to gain knowledge. Upon reaching some level of expertise, the inclination to coast along increases. Becoming complacent is a common temptation throughout life; however, becoming complacent in the intellectual area is risky to the survival of an organization or the relevance of an individual.

For those who want to learn, there are basically five ways to go about it:

First is learning through sources—simply find a teacher or book on a subject and learn from those sources. This is the most common of learning techniques, but there are others.

The second is through experience, where we place less of an emphasis on the abstract and more on live practice. This is a very powerful way to learn, but it can also be painful and expensive.

Third is reflection, where we research, investigate, and meditate on a concept before acting. For example, the reflective learner would not just launch a website and hope for the best, but would carefully study all of the options, seek feedback, examine other websites, design the content, develop their marketing plan, and refine their concepts.

Fourth is modeling, where one seeks answers by configuring diagrams, pictures, or "mind mapping" to achieve the best approach. This can be effective as it incorporates the visual aspects of learning.

Fifth is trial and error or seeing what works and what doesn't. Little or no time is used in reading the "owners manual." This is a method of finding a satisfactory solution by testing various alternatives, eliminating failures, and building upon successes. Thomas Edison used this approach for inventing the light bulb.

But learning in any form is hard work. In fact, Dr. Martin Luther King, Jr., said "Nothing pains some people more than having to think." Left Line people are ignorant, but often believe they know everything and that they are above the learning process.

The only thing more expensive than education is ignorance.

The JonBenet Ramsey Case: "Keystone Cop" *Ignorance*

On December 26, 1997, a seven-year-old girl, JonBenet Ramsey, was reported kidnaped from her home in Boulder, Colorado. Her body was later found in the home's basement. Police initially focused on her parents as potential suspects. The crime is still unsolved and evidence suggests that her parents were actually not involved.

When the Ramseys wanted to sell their Boulder home, I was asked by local realtors to advise the couple on the impact of crime-scene stigma. Before I consulted on the project, I had two conditions:

First, I had made some comments about the Ramseys that had been quoted in *The Denver Post.* They needed to be aware of them, because they were not entirely complimentary.

Second, in lieu of a fee, I asked that a donation be made to the Nicole Brown Charitable Foundation. I had no desire to profit from a crime like this.

With those conditions met, I consulted on the project.

During the course of the assignment I heard some comments from those who were far more involved with the case. Like anybody, I've wondered if the parents had committed the crime and, at this point, I still have no idea.

One would be hard-pressed, however, to find poorer police work than what was done by the Boulder Police Department. As an occasional viewer of crime-solving documentaries, even *I* know that a crime scene must be sealed off. When the Boulder police arrived at the Ramsey house, it was presumably the scene of a kidnapping where the kidnapper had entered the house. How could any cop be so inept as to not empty the house for a forensic examination?

What kind of instruction and schooling do the police in Boulder undergo? Clearly, the department had given little weight to basic police training. The improper action in the Ramsey case illustrates how proper training and an ongoing respect for learning is an absolute requirement. This responsibility is *never* complete.

We might never know if the Ramsey parents were involved in their daughter's murder because of the negligent contamination of

The Jon Benet Ramsey house in Boulder, Colorado.

the crime scene. Likewise, if John and Patsy Ramsey were *not* involved, they have suffered irreparable harm from the inept investigation.

Great minds have always respected education and learning

Henry Ford said, "Anyone who stops learning is old, whether at twenty or eighty. Anyone who keeps learning stays young. The greatest thing in life is to keep your mind young."

Winston Churchill added, "Personally, I'm always ready to learn, although I do not always like being taught."

Thinking isn't always easy. In fact, many people prefer *not* to think. Earl Nightingale took that reality one step further when he stated, "Most people would rather *die* than think!"

A Formal Education Is Invaluable

I must admit that I was once guilty of a Left Line attitude myself. Eager to take on the business world, I left college just one elective short of my bachelor's degree to pursue a high-tech opportunity in Silicon Valley. I considered myself an intense entrepreneur.

Here's how the trial-by-error tale progressed:

"Adapting to Change" Journey

Learning new ideas and worthwhile concepts can be difficult. At first, external influences can result in denial and then personal resistance. Depending upon the character of the person, "open mindedness" and exploration will prevail and lead to eventual acceptance.

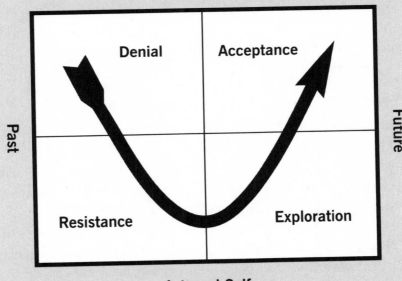

Knowledge Acquisition Segments
by Neil Balholm
Comteam Consulting

We started by importing computers from Asia, which was initially successful, but the change of technology was swift and our product became obsolete overnight.

So . . . we developed one of the world's first portable computers, which had a small cathode-ray type monitor the size of a small suitcase. We were certain *this* time we were leading the way . . . until the flat screens wiped that idea out.

So . . . we moved into software. We developed office automation software for dentists and doctors, but came to the sad realization that, at that time, there were some things the computer couldn't replace, the paper calendar being one of them.

Even with all the climbs and falls, we never had a problem getting investor money and even went public. We were later acquired and the investors tripled their investment. In the process, however, I realized I had a lot to learn. I went back to college to complete my one last elective unit, and then went on to graduate school. I've had a business career with a *lack* of education and one *with* an education.

I prefer the latter.

"If You Can't Convince Them, Confuse Them"

Because I research disasters that often cause tremendous damage, I have testified as an expert witness on dozens of occasions. It is annoying to know the truth of an issue, only to see it clouded by spin-doctor lawyers. This sometimes results in absolutely ridiculous jury decisions. As frustrating as it may be, lawyers are trained to "spin," and a really good attorney can effectively argue both sides of a case. But for some attorneys, the truth has a very limited role to play. When the facts are not very good for their case, many attorneys follow Harry S. Truman's advice, "If you can't convince them, confuse them."

To compound the problem, our legal system assumes that our juries possess certain experience and intelligence that they just do not have. This *very* incorrect assumption was exposed to the public with the O. J. Simpson murder trial decision.

While I have seen some astounding jury decisions, I do *not* believe that people on juries are stupid. Indeed, I think many jurors are quite bright. But *there is nothing more ignorant than intelligent people trying to make decisions on topics they're not familiar with*. If a brain surgeon is forced to deal with a case involving automobile mechanics, it's easy to spin, confuse, and confound the surgeon. Conversely, an intelligent automobile mechanic might be just as easily confounded and "spun" on the topic of medicine in a malpractice claim.

It is said that the "greatest legal minds" comprise the U.S. Supreme Court, yet there is often bitter disagreement and dissent between the nine justices themselves. If this is true for the best legal minds, what chance does a jury have of rendering an intelligent legal verdict when it has absolutely no training or background in the matters being disputed? The outcome of *any* lawsuit is uncertain and, in some cases, approaches randomness.

The answer to this dilemma is simple. Juries could be composed of blue ribbon panelists who have a professional background in the topic being disputed, whether it's medicine, business, real estate, technology, and so forth. At least *then* a plaintiff or defendant can have a reasonable chance of obtaining an intelligent decision.

While this is a painfully obvious solution, it will likely never happen. The less-than-perfect system in place provides a fertile ground for profitable lawsuits, so its implementation would eliminate a lot of profit.

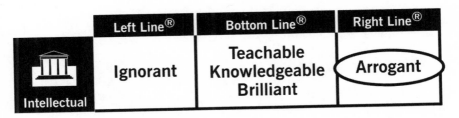

	Left Line®	Bottom Line®	Right Line®
Intellectual	Ignorant	Teachable Knowledgeable Brilliant	Arrogant

Arrogance Can Negate Intelligence

As strange as it may sound, past success can play a significant role in setting someone up for failure. A long run of accomplishments can create overconfidence and the assumption that everything must automatically result in success. A genuine achiever, no matter how many achievements they have stacked up, will always remain "teachable" and "stay on their toes."

While training and education are essential, they still do not guarantee intelligent behavior. Many "super-educated" people make horrible Right Line mistakes.

In upstate New York, the Love Canal was given its name by a nineteenth-century industrialist, Colonel William T. Love. In 1893, he started construction of a ten-mile canal from Lake Erie to Lake Ontario. The plan was that the 110-foot drop would bypass Niagara Falls and the resulting hydropower would produce direct electricity to power the new "model city."

With the technology of the day, the city needed to be right next to the source of power. Only about a mile of the canal was dug before the project was abandoned due to the discovery of alternating current, which could travel long distances over power lines.

The canal filled with rainwater and became a local swimming hole in the summer and an ice rink in the winter. Then, during World War II, Hooker Chemical Company and others dumped 21,800 tons

The Love Canal Treatment Facility is a fenced area that is about a mile long.

Hundreds of deserted homes line the Love Canal.

of toxic chemicals, including acid chlorides, sulfur compounds, TCPs and benzyl alcohol into the canal. At the end of the war, they covered up the canal and left.

Meanwhile, the local area was prospering and the demand for land increased. The school district approached Hooker Chemical, asking for the land to use for schools and housing.

Initially, Hooker said "no" because of obvious environmental issues. But after unrelenting pressure from the district, Hooker sold the land to the local school board, along with a bold warning that *nothing should be developed on the old canal site*.

The sales price? One dollar.

In one of the most incredible and irresponsible decisions in environmental history, the school board—which was *loaded* with PhDs—chose to ignore the warnings and built the 99th Street Elementary School directly on top of the old, covered canal. In fact, the schoolyard literally straddled the site.

Further, in the 1950s, hundreds of middle-class homes were built along both sides of the canal area.

In the 1970s, local residents became alarmed at health problems, sludge, and fumes, and the Love Canal Homeowner's Association became very vocal. On August 7, 1978, President Jimmy Carter declared a federal state of emergency, and the government offered to pay full-price for 789 homes.

This school board's decision shows that education does not equal intelligence.

When one considers the school board's mandate to respect the educational process, along with its responsibly for teaching the community's children, the entire incident is even more astounding.

The school board's members certainly had a high level of education, but they were hardly intelligent. Apparently believing that they were above the warnings of the chemical company, the school board did what only the truly ignorant would do.

Add in an extra twist: Hooker Chemical was sued, while the school board was not! The attorney for the chemical company—now named Occidental—told me that their winning defense involved simply pointing to the original $1 sale with its attached "hazardous waste" warning to the school board. Occidental won the lawsuit, but, to this day, the school board has never had to answer for its Right Line arrogance.

Intelligent People Are Always *Teachable*

After his first day of first grade, my son, Michael, asked me, "Dad, I really love school. How old do you get when you are done learning?"

It's an intriguing question because *many people have the attitude that once they are past a certain point, their education and learning is complete*. My reply was that someday we may finish high school and college, but we never finish our education. In fact, the vast majority of college graduates end up in a field that has nothing to do with their major. I've used the Schools vs. Ongoing Training chart to illustrate that, even if an individual takes every course offered at college, there's an entire array of additional subjects needed for continued professional development.

Schools vs. Ongoing Training

While formal schools and college provide an outstanding foundation, the learning process continues well past graduation. In fact, a principle benefit of college is to learn research and study skills to be applied throughout life.

This chart outlines an array of college classes, but the right column shows the continuing education needed over a career.

		School Education	Continuing Education
PURPOSE	Philosophical	Philosophy Religion Psychology	Mission Statement Corporate Culture
	Intellectual	Engineering Math Statistics Education Computer Science	Employee Orientation Train the Trainer Systems
PEOPLE	Sociological	Sociology Humanities Law Child Development	Team Building Diversity Leadership Hiring Firing Job Descriptions Competitive Advantage
	Influential	English Literature Communications Marketing Art Music Photography Theatre	Negotiation Advertising
PRODUCTIVITY	Physical	Physical Ed Health Chemistry Cooking Dance Biology Medicine Physics	Employee fitness Product Development Quality Control
	Environmental	Architecture Botany Geography Geology Interior Design Engineering	Office Management Facility Management The Paperless Office
	Financial	Accounting Finance Economics	Pricing Cost Cutting
PROGRESS	Developmental	Business Management Orgizational Behavior	Goal Setting Strategic Planning Problem Solving
	Operational	Computer Science Travel	Time Management Crisis Management Systems
	Consequential	History Genealogy Humanities Anthropology	Incentive Programs Employee Reviews

Even if an educated person continues to invest in classes and seminars, he should always remain on guard against being qualified for a world that no longer exists. Each day, we are faced with new situations that require us to be continuously learning.

"The difference between being educated and uneducated is the same difference as being alive and being dead." —Aristotle

There are a number of relatively simple actions we can take that can keep us informed. As individuals, we should always ask ourselves, "Am I teachable and actively learning new things?" Our education can always continue through traveling, trips to museums, reading and even surfing the Internet.

In business, we should regularly ask ourselves, "Are we actively training and learning as a team?" This is accomplished through continuing education, updating our technical and computer skills and being involved with sales and customer service training.

There is only one thing worse than training people and losing them, and that is not training people . . . and keeping them.

One of the easiest learning skills lies in *identifying unproductive time and making it productive.* As an example, I live in the Los Angeles suburbs, so I spend a lot of time in the car. I try to do three things when I'm in my car:

1. It's a great time to talk to people. One attorney friend told me that he makes calls in the car and bills more than $2,000 a week ($100,000 a year) from his car-based cell phone conversations.
2. I keep a small tape recorder handy to dictate notes or my journal.
3. I also have CDs of books or lectures that I regularly listen to.

If we are not progressing, we are regressing. If we are not getting smarter, we are becoming ignorant.

Intelligence—not IQ—has a big market value. Those who understand this give themselves tremendous advantage.

Sharing *Knowledge* Correctly

In a single semester at business school, I observed the quintessential example of terrible vs. outstanding displays of knowledge.

First, there was the professor who was well-published and well-known, but he scared the heck out of us. He would assign volumes of texts to read, including—of course—the one he had written. During the class, he would ask a question like, "If the author of book A said this, and book B said that, what do you suppose the author of book C would say about it?" Then he would call on someone in the class.

He was careful to always ask the question . . . and *then* call on the person, so that everyone was on edge for every question. The atmosphere was tense. Everyone was terrified. I immediately and happily forgot everything the minute the class was over. *Sure, this professor was knowledgeable and certainly proved as much in his overbearing way, but the class was ultimately a waste of time.*

Then there was another professor, who was voted the "Best Professor of the Year." He didn't really lecture the class, but rather facilitated an outstanding discussion. He would draw thoughts and experiences out of the class and interweave them with the course materials. The discussions had sufficient discipline that if anyone made a comment that was off topic, the professor would step in and pull the class back into sync. The conversations were so stimulating that I would leave the classroom with a mental buzz. *This professor wasn't concerned about proving his knowledge; his only focus was in getting us to think and reason in a real world.*

No Amount of Knowledge Matters if It Is Not Used Correctly

I grew up down the street from one of the brightest kids I had ever known. While I struggled with many classes, it all came easily to him. He knew everything and he barely studied at all.

I remember being stuck on an algebra problem for hours and eventually swallowing my pride and going down the street to ask him for help. He had not read the chapter or even started his homework, but he immediately knew the answer to my question. He had to explain the problem to me about three times before I got it.

One might expect great things from such a gifted child . . . but this one went to jail.

An average person who does something productive with his knowledge is more intelligent than a genius who does nothing.

Simple Techniques Can Maximize Your Knowledge

Irrespective of one's natural aptitude, a few basic rules can increase your knowledge and subsequent "intelligence" tremendously:

1. The Mother of Learning Is Repetition

I learned this as a Boy Scout. When I was at a Scout jamboree, we had a class on packing our backpacks. The instructor was covering all kinds of material, none of which I could recount today. Then he said something that stuck. He said, "Now, SCOUTS! When packing, never, never, never, never, never, never, never, never, never, never, never forget . . . to always pack everything in small plastic bags!"

When I got back to camp, I told our scoutmaster about this strange teacher and how he had repeated himself ten or twelve times.

My scoutmaster replied, "Well, you haven't forgotten have you?"

Today, I can't remember any of my Boy Scout knots or much of anything else I learned; but because of that repetitive phrase, I never forget to use plastic bags when packing a backpack, a habit I have continued today each time I pack my suitcase.

2. Take Notes!

When listening to a speaker or when sitting in a meeting, taking notes is critical. The action of hearing something in your ear, that then travels down your spine, down your arm, into your hand and onto paper, greatly increases your absorption of that information.

Sometimes when I am in a meeting or listening to a great speaker, I often look around and am amazed that I'm the only one taking notes. If you just sit and listen, your retention is less than 20

Johari Window Model

"Open Area" knowledge has little value, but every effort should be made to acquire "blind area" knowledge where others know something that you do not. One should also make an effort to share "Hidden Area" knowledge with others where appropriate.

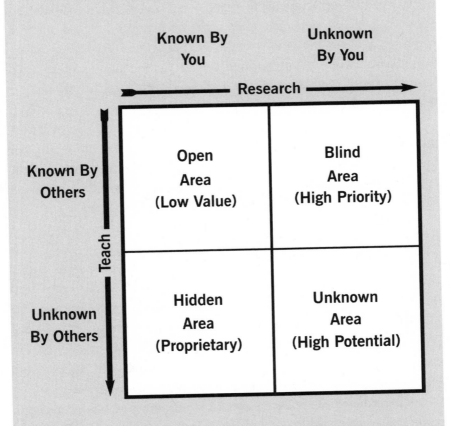

Adapted from the Ingham and Luft Johari Window

percent a few days later. When you take notes, however, retention at least doubles, even if you never look at your notes again.

When you *do* review your notes, your retention goes up to about 50 percent.

If you take notes, and then share the concepts with another person—effectively becoming a teacher—your retention of the material will go up to well over 75 percent.

3. Dalai Lama: "Share Your Knowledge!"

Once I had a private conversation with a top partner of one of the world's largest consulting firms. I told him that I had developed some specialized methodologies in my field, and that I was teaching seminars around the country and writing a book on the subject. I was startled when he questioned this tactic and suggested that, if I had a proprietary methodology, I should keep it to myself and not tell anyone about it.

He could not have been more wrong. As far as my career goes, publishing these methods was one of the smartest moves I made. The feedback and insight I received from teaching seminars around the country was invaluable, and the opportunities I received would never have come without the book being published.

Brilliance Is a Trait Anyone Can Acquire

I grew up in Southern California where elementary school ended with the sixth grade. On my first day of junior high, I was stunned to learn that my old sixth grade teacher had recommended that I be placed in the remedial math class. Granted, this teacher had not ranked among my favorites, and, being the goof-off that I was, I'm sure the feeling was mutual. Nonetheless, I was a decent student, and I felt insulted to have been placed in the remedial math class.

I immediately went to my school counselor, Mr. Moore, to complain. I told him that I liked math and should be moved up. I expected Mr. Moore to place me in the main level math class where the majority of students were, but for some reason, he put me in the advanced math class. To this day, I don't know if this was intentional or an accident, but there I was, in the advanced math class with all the school "brains."

At first, I was tempted to return to Mr. Moore and tell him that he had over-compensated for my problem, but I decided to stay and give it a try. I was not the brightest student in the advanced math class, but I held my own. Because I did well, I was labeled an "advanced student" from that point forward, which placed me in the advanced classes for math, physics, and biology through the rest of junior high and high school. Not only did I complete high school classes that gave me college credit, but other students regarded me as being bright.

Little did they know of the roots of this "advanced student."

Take Responsibility for Your Own Brilliance

My experience has taught me that a "brilliant mind" is really more a way of thinking than the outgrowth of shear aptitude. This point was brought home when my son, Michael, was in third grade.

Michael had completed second grade by scoring in the ninety-eighth percentile nationally in mathematics. When he entered third grade, he was placed in a second-third grade combination class. While these arrangements might be acceptable in some situations, as parents we were unimpressed. The teacher was overwhelmed in a classroom with such a wide range of ages and academic aptitudes. Michael's test scores fell like a rock. My wife and I had had enough. We went to the principal and demanded that he be removed. By this time, three months of the school year had gone by and Michael was losing ground fast.

I snapped into action.

Rather than coming home from work to have dinner and relax, I got a pack of multiplication flash cards and started going through them with Michael. I made every effort to make the flash card drills fun. If he missed an answer, it was not a big deal; I just showed him the answer and stuck the card back into the deck.

Within just two weeks, he went from fumbling around to ripping right through the entire pack. My younger son, Steve, who was in second grade, watched this process. He wanted in on the action and asked that I go through the flash cards with him. While this was well beyond where he should have been academically, I went through the cards and remarkably, he got the hang of it in just a few nights. Then my four-year old daughter had to join the party, and she learned some of the simpler cards, one year before kindergarten.

I'm not one of those parents who thinks my kids are geniuses. The point is this:

> *"Intelligence" can be taught, as long as one remains teachable.*
> *"Brilliance" can be acquired when you understand that anyone*
> *can obtain it.*

With just a little effort, my kids zoomed beyond their expected "intelligence" levels. With some extra effort, higher expectations and fun, their academic accomplishments soared.

The same can be true for most anyone.

I've had the opportunity to meet and work with thousands of people in a wide variety of careers. I've seen some remarkable intellectual strengths, such as engineers who design things that help millions of people, or executives who are able to position their companies at the top of an industry.

I've also discovered that everyone has a "knowledge gap" and has the capacity to build their intellect in some way. The engineer may be promoted to run a department, but then learns that they do not have the "people skills" necessary to be effective. The executive may be brilliant with a marketing plan, but have dismal results in building a team. The bottom line is that the opportunity for improvement exists with every person and within every organization. Every achiever must have a deliberate plan and invest the time to continuously learn more.

Intellectual Insights

- The only thing worse than paying for employee training and losing them, is providing no training and *keeping* them.
- Be teachable. Know-it-alls slam the door in the face of opportunity.
- Nobody is above being "teachable."
- Nothing is more painful for some people than having to think.
- The day we finish our learning is the day we finish our living.
- Intelligence can be learned.
- Anyone who stops learning is, by definition, old.
- We can greatly advance our learning by using educational tapes when we drive.
- A mistake or tragedy, large or small, always yields a great learning experience.
- The best teachers draw on the knowledge of the classroom, rather than lecturing to it.
- Take notes. The process of letting a message come in our ears, down our arms and out to our hand greatly amplifies the learning experience.
- The highest pinnacle of learning is reached when we teach a concept to another person.
- Repetition is the mother of learning.
- We live in a world of thirty- and sixty-minute television solutions. Real solutions require patience and the delay of gratification.

Part II

People

People is founded in the Latin *populus*, meaning "population" or a "body of persons" comprising a "community," or a "host of warriors" acting upon character, personal power, influence and the destiny of men. "People" are the ultimate creation and thus they are the ultimate priority. "People" includes both "Sociological" and "Influential" issues.

Chapter Three

Sociological

Think: Team Sport

No great achievement has ever been the efforts of just one person. Effective partnering is critical to success, and partnering with those with complementary skills creates a dynamic synergy. Being empathetic to others' points of view and personality types makes the team perform better.

People need people. Many might take that for granted, but science has actually proven that people cannot successfully live alone. In fact, one of the harshest punishments in prison is simple solitary confinement. It drives men mad.

Understanding personality types is an effective tool in team building. By identifying your personality type and those of others, we see where everyone's strengths fit in. Weaknesses can be viewed more objectively, rather than taken personally. Everyone can build on strengths, while identifying those issues to keep an eye on.

Team dynamics determine the direction of an organization. Effective team members tend to be encouraging, more models and less critics. They value differences, diversity, and what everyone brings to the game. Good teams build relationships and widen their sphere of influence with people of character and with those they can trust. Tasks are delegated to the right person. They help others who are weaker than themselves and graciously accept help and feedback when they need it. Ideal teams are efficient and competitive, but when the "whistle blows," they are good sports and help their competition up off the field.

For people to live and work with each other successfully, there must be defined roles and responsibilities whether they exist within families, companies, or society as a whole. When roles and responsibilities are defined and adhered to, conflict is at a minimum and achievement is at its highest; however, problems are created when people fail to meet their sociological responsibilities.

Why the Titanic Shouldn't Have Sunk

The movie *Titanic* was a great success in the theaters. It won the Academy Award® for Best Picture and made a fortune at the box office. Like millions of others, I enjoyed most of the movie, but I was disappointed that it omitted many fascinating key historic facts while focusing mainly on a fictional story. Of these facts, the most interesting is that *all the passengers and crew came excruciatingly close to actually being rescued.*

Another ocean liner, the *Californian*, was stopped for the night only nineteen miles away and within easy eyesight of the *Titanic*. Passengers and the crew of the *Californian* watched the white emergency flares go off on the Titanic, but they weren't sure if the flares were meant to signal an emergency, or if the crew and passengers were firing flares in celebration of the maiden voyage. They watched as the ship appeared to be sailing off into the horizon, but actually the ship was listing and sinking.

Nevertheless, the crew thought that if the ship really was in trouble, its own crew would have sent a radio message, and no such message had been received. At 11:05 p.m., the *Californian* radioman, Cyril Evans, sent a message, but was abruptly cut off by the Titanic radioman who was frantically communicating with Cape Race. Rather than listen to those communications, Evans turned off his radio and went to sleep. Had he stayed awake to monitor the transmissions as his responsibilities mandated, the loss of life from the *Titanic* would have been minimal, if at all.

The radioman failed in his responsibilities to simply stay awake. As a result, hundreds of people aboard the Titanic died.

TEAM Personality Chart

Personality typing originated with the historical work of the "Four Humours" of Hippocrates (c. 400 BC), and later refined by Aristotle (c. 325 BC), Galen (c. 190 AD), Paracelsus (c. 1550 AD) and others. The TEAM Personality chart incorporates early works, along with contemporary works of Troy L. Tate, the author of *The DNA of Successful Leaders*, as well as some of nature's examples that originate from the work of Dr. Gary Smalley.

This personality chart is useful for identifying one's primary and secondary personality traits. Note that it takes all four personality types to build a complete team:

Personality Type	T	E	A	M
Dominant Trait (Four Humours)	Take Charge (Choleric)	Enjoyment (Sanguine)	Ally (Phlegmatic)	Meticulous (Melancholic)
Job Description	CEO, Manager, Entrepreneur Trial Lawyer, Quarterback	Sales, Host, Entertainer, Mascot, Cheerleader	Teacher, Administrator, Line Worker, Player	CPA, Doctor, Engineer, Coach
Nature	Lion, Eagle, Queen Bee	Otter, Dolphin	Golden Retriever, Hamster	Beaver, Chipmunk, Army Ant
Car	Flashy, Powerful	Party Bus, Convertible	SUV, Truck, Jeep	Anything Practical
Color	Red	Yellow	Aqua	Blue
Typical Strengths	Leader, Visionary, Aggressive, Competitive, Decision Maker	Fun, Positive, Social, Motivating, Lots of Friends	Devoted, Listener, Caring, Calm, Accommodating, Encouraging	Detail-Oriented, Organized, Exactness, Creative, Respect, Order
Typical Weaknesses	Puts Projects Over People, Domineering, Blunt	Superficial, Lack Follow-Up, Goof Off, Permissive, Lack Discipline	Resists Change, Too Sensitive, Too Soft, Lethargic	Perfectionist, Inflexible, Critical, Unrealistic, Pessimistic

As one military leader said, "The brave man who is inattentive or negligent to his duty is worth little more than the coward who deserts in the hour of danger."

Illicit Action Often Stems from an Illogical Belief in One's Importance

Most of us don't think of the United States as a colonial power, because the U.S. government does not typically have an agenda of exploiting people. In fact, such imperialistic notions are upsetting to most Americans. While I'm patriotic, I must acknowledge that the U.S. government has, at times, participated in Left Line illicit behavior that would make our forefathers blush.

On March 1, 1954, the U.S. descended on the Marshall Islands and, with little thought for its inhabitants, detonated dozens of nuclear bombs. This included the infamous Bravo test on the Bikini Atoll, a string of several tiny islands that circle a twenty-four-mile lagoon. Bravo was the largest atmospheric nuclear explosion in history, with an explosive force equal to nearly one thousand Hiroshima-type bombs. It vaporized the test island, parts of two other islands, and left a mile-wide crater in the lagoon floor.

I have done a great deal of work for the Nuclear Claims Tribunal. When I conducted aerial surveys of the Bravo Crater site on Bikini, I saw a nearly perfect circular crater in deep blue tropical waters. Littered all around Bikini are similar smaller craters from other blasts—the entire area looks something like a tropical moon. In total, nearly seventy acres of the Bikini Atoll were vaporized by nuclear testing.

The Marshall Islands Were an Innocent Paradise

The Marshall Islands are a fragile place. I noticed on my first visit that there is a nearly immeasurable distinction between sea and land. There are no hills, mountains or valleys anywhere. The average elevation is about seven feet above sea level. As we crossed a small bridge in the capital city of Majaro, I was told that it was the highest point in the country.

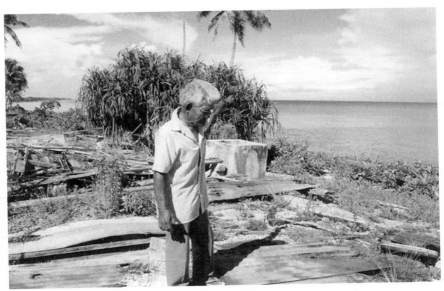

Standing on the site of his former home,
John points in the direction of the nuclear tests.

Land is scarce; the total land area of the country totals about seventy square miles, which is spread over 375,000 square miles of ocean. The atolls themselves consist of a series of islands and reefs that surround a lagoon. In many areas, there is a small, two-lane road with houses on either side, and the houses themselves front either the lagoon or the ocean. Indeed, in many areas the island is so narrow that I was able to throw a rock from the ocean side to the lagoon side.

In my entire life, I have never caught anything bigger than an eight-inch trout. But in the Marshall Islands, I felt like the editor-in-chief of Field & Stream.

In one quick fishing trip before breakfast, I caught two 3-foot tunas and a shark, which I carefully released.

Walking along the beach, I picked up more shells than you could find in all the tourist shops of La Jolla, and I found a giant clamshell so large that even two of us couldn't pick it up. I found two more clamshells that weighed in at about fifty pounds each, and I brought one home at the invitation of the owners of the islands.

The United States' weapons testing program turned this island paradise into a nuclear war zone.

As a diver, I had seen plenty of moray eels, but I had never seen such a virgin place where they slept and played right on the shoreline. I followed sea turtle tracks on the sand right up to their nests. I saw schools of thousands of bright tropical fish that cost forty-five dollars each at the pet store at home. The coconut crabs were fascinating. They're the world's largest land crustacean—looking something like a lobster—but they climb coconut trees, cut the coconuts off the branches and then climb down and eat them by husking the shell with their claws.

The people who inhabit the Marshall Islands, like their environment, are calm and quite friendly. I had the privilege of accompanying many of the landowners and local people to Rongelap and Rongerik, where much of the nuclear fallout came down. I will never forget my conversations with John, an elderly man who stood on his former home site with me in Rongelap and recalled the day the Bravo nuclear test was conducted.

He had gotten up early to make coffee, and the sun had not yet come up. Suddenly, the sky lit up like it was day. He could see the

Two and a half islands that once sat here were vaporized
by the nuclear test that left this mile wide "Bravo Crater."

large mushroom cloud rising off the horizon from Bikini and, soon
after, he felt the blast of the shock wave on his face and saw waves
breaking in the otherwise calm lagoon.

Later, as the entire village woke up, they watched the radioactive
gray ash fall on them . . . their houses . . . their children.

John is a calm and kind man. He did not express any anger, only
deep sorrow that his one-year-old daughter died from leukemia
soon after Bravo.

Illicit Acts Occur When the Offender Loses Sight of the Bigger Picture

In recently declassified documents from the U.S. Government,
I've learned that not only did the military scientists know about the
high level of radioactivity on Rongelap, but *they were pleased to have the*
chance to study the long-term impact of radioactivity on humans.

In 1994, U.S. Congressman George Miller wrote, "Some Ronge-
lapese have said they believe they were used as guinea pigs to further

U.S. understanding of the effects of radiation on humans. In light of recent disclosures regarding actual radiation experimentation in the United States during this period, that possibility cannot be ignored."

Congressman Miller also commented on an ongoing thyroid study in the Marshalls. "The findings of the thyroid survey are disturbing. The Committee has been informed that even if only 50 percent of the survey results are verified . . . *the [thyroid cancer] incidence rate is still significantly higher, by a factor of 100, than the rate of thyroid cancer found anywhere else in the world.*"

U.S. Representatives George Miller and Ron de Lugo wrote: "There is no doubt that the AEC (Atomic Energy Commission) intentionally returned (Marshallese) to islands which it considered to be 'by far the most contaminated places in the world,' but which, it told the people, were safe. Nor is there any doubt that the AEC, through the Brookhaven National Laboratory, then *planned and conducted test after test on these people to study their bodies' reaction to life in that contaminated environment.*"

In other words, islanders were purposely resettled on contaminated islands so that the U.S. Government could study the long-term effects of radiation on people. Hard to imagine, isn't it?

The U.S. Government had social roles and responsibilities that not only weren't met, but were blatantly *neglected* in the Marshall Island operations. Detonating nuclear devices near inhabited islands is wildly stupid. But to knowingly move people back onto contaminated islands is illicit. As a result, billions of dollars were lost, and many innocent lives were harmed or lost.

These Island People Proved Stronger Than the "Superpower"

While traveling to the Marshall Islands and meeting with dozens of the victims who had lost children or become sick themselves, I was surprised that none of them seemed particularly angry. Indeed, they were remarkably calm. In the aftermath of being showered with nuclear fallout and suffering all types of radioactive-related diseases, their attitudes were exactly the opposite of what one would expect.

They apparently understood that getting irate would not change the past. They dealt with the problems with dignity and realized, as Winston Churchill said, that "Nothing is more costly, nothing is more sterile, than vengeance." They also proved themselves the stronger party, as Mahatma Gandhi once said, "The weak can never forgive. Forgiveness is the attribute of the strong."

The Worst of the Worst: Child Molesters

I believe the worst example of illicit behavior in all of society involves child molesters.

In June 1994, in the Hamilton Township of western New Jersey, seven-year old Megan Kanka crossed the street to visit a friend. On the way, she stopped to talk to Jesse Timmendequas, who was washing his car in the driveway. The community was not aware that he was a twice-convicted child molester who had served six years of a ten-year sentence and lived with two other convicted molesters that he'd met in prison. Timmendequas molested and murdered the young girl, for which he was convicted and sentenced to the death penalty.

The community banded together to purchase the house where little Megan Kanka was murdered, and turned the site into a park.

The neighborhood was outraged that *three convicted child molesters could live near dozens of families with no notice.* From that outrage, Congress passed a 1996 federal law requiring states to initiate some form of public notification of convicted child molesters living in local neighborhoods. Today, this is known as Megan's Law, which provides parents of young children a better chance to create barriers against those who are prone to this type of illicit behavior.

I will never forget meeting Megan's mother, Maureen Kanka, and having the opportunity to speak with her in detail about the entire incident. She did not allow this unimaginable tragedy to destroy her, but rather channeled her grief into activities that would help others to not have to pass through the same tragedy.

Mrs. Kanka worked on an agenda to pass federal legislation to notify the community when sex offenders lived nearby. *The idea was not to notify parents so that they would know which house to throw eggs at, but rather to give parents the information they need to steer their kids away from potential danger, and from people who certainly compete with their family's best interests.* Since our visit, her agenda has become federal and international law.

I remember telling Mrs. Kanka that I simply could not imagine the grief she and her family had felt, and she answered, "No, you don't want to know what this is like; I wouldn't wish it on my worst enemy." Her ability to move forward in the face of such a tremendous tragedy—and to even help others—is exemplary.

In reviewing a case as upsetting as the one involving Megan, it's easy to see that it really is not be desirable for *everyone* to "win." *For parents, child molesters and drug dealers are competition.* I personally have no interest in seeing child molesters or drug dealers enjoy any level of success. In fact, I want them to lose in the worst way.

If We Think Everyone Can Win, We've All Crossed the *Annoying* Right Line

During a trip to Michigan to give a lecture, I saw an exhibit in my hotel that featured a book for elementary children titled, *Everybody*

Wins! I thought to myself, "What a joke! That doesn't even remotely resemble anything in real life!"

I like the "win-win" concept most of the time. Certainly, we want many of those around us to win, but this simply does not work all the time in real life. Do football teams think win-win? Of course not. Obviously, the objective in football is to beat the opposition.

While any eighth-grade lineman knows he needs to beat the competition, the business world of grown-ups seems to forget this same truth. While many are at least superficially attracted to the idea of "everybody winning," the theory in itself has clear flaws.

Whether reviewing a case as upsetting as the Kankas' or simply watching a football game, it is easy to see that *everyone can't win*. I'm not suggesting that our day-to-day competition is on a par with drug dealers or child molesters, but the same concept *does* apply to our business deals. In real life, we simply want our families, businesses, and society to win and competitors to lose.

Let's face it, a better slogan than "win-win" would be "team sport."

Bottom Line Success Also Has Room for *Leniency*

My son Drake is only four years old, but he is a smart kid. He can diffuse even the most perilous situations with his charm. Once he was misbehaving, and my wife, Melanie, said, "Drake, when are you going to behave?" to which he replied, "Not yet!" My wife laughed so hard that he once again walked for his crimes.

As seniors in high school, my friends and I spent a considerable amount of time thinking of what we could do to break the rules and amuse ourselves with various pranks. We made many attempts and had several successes, but our supreme accomplishment was what we called "fire-extinguishing." This exercise would start by first getting a fire extinguisher, filling it with water and then using the tire hose at the gas station to pressurize it. Then, we'd drive around squirting people.

At the time, the movie, *Jaws* was drawing large lines at the local theater. Our goal was to squirt every person in the entire line. We learned that one fire extinguisher would not do the trick, so we acquired several more and returned to the next showing where we *did* meet our goal. We were greatly amused by our success.

Hungry from our activities, we headed for dinner at the drive-through and squirted the guy at the window. Swaggering with *that* success, we then got the brilliant idea to put a fire extinguisher up one of the guy's jackets with the hose down his arm. He walked into the restaurant and squirted all the patrons.

The next day at school, an announcement came over the loud speaker asking that a short list of individuals meet at the principal's office. Oddly, that list of individuals matched exactly those in the car the night before.

While I joked with my friends as we walked down the hall, I was scared. I went trembling to the principal's office where I had the opportunity to meet with Detective Johnson of the Fullerton Police Department. I had heard that "confession was good for the soul," so I quickly admitted my part of the crime. He asked for my dad's work phone number. (I immediately wondered what was supposed to be so good about confession.) He then told me that he would give me a day to tell my dad myself before he called him.

He knew that I was going to have a bad night.

When I went home, I was terrified. I sat in my room with a big pit in my stomach. I was shaking. I knew I was dead. I finally told my older brother my dilemma, and he told me to just get it over with.

I walked into the kitchen and said, "Dad, I gotta tell you something," and then I spilled the beans. Expecting to be grounded for life, I'll never forget his reply: "Randy, I'm really mad . . . that sounds like you had a lot of fun, and I'm mad that you didn't invite me to go with you!" Then he laughed.

By simply watching me slink into the kitchen and by listening carefully as I poured out my tale, my dad knew that I had already been through enough. My dad could have pounded me with a harsh punishment, but he could see that I'd never be so stupid again. To this day, I remember that lesson when I'm dealing with my own kids' transgressions.

More than once, I have broken traffic laws and been pulled over by the police, only to be let off the hook. I have been stupid and broken other rules throughout my growing-up years, and many times people have given me a break.

Society has laws.

Companies have policies.

Parents have boundaries.

Religions have commandments.

Organizations have rules.

Under-regulation results in chaos and over-regulation results in resentment. The challenge is to find a balance, and that often comes with experience.

Rules are essential, but even good people will mess up once in a while. Some of the harshest punishments will not come from those we might have offended, but from ourselves. It's okay to make mistakes once in a while, as long as we learn and keep the lessons.

The Jarrell Tornado was a rare "F5" and wiped out much of the town.

Every home on this street was ripped out by the tornado,
but rebuilding has begun.

Acting *Lawfully* Also Means Respecting the Laws Of Nature

Sometimes nature makes the rules, and few are as frightening as a tornado. The Jarrell Tornado in Williamson County, Texas, was considered one of history's worst.

Following a warning at 3:30 PM, on May 27, 1997, at 3:42 PM, a tornado hit with winds over 261 mph. This was an extremely rare event, as the Fujita Scale for tornado strength classifications ranked it as an F5 (defined as "incredible" with wind speeds between 261 and 318 mph). Virtually everything in the path of the tornado was destroyed. Trees were debarked and uprooted, grass was pulled from the ground, three hundred head of cattle were lost, and dozens of cars were thrown more than half a mile.

Residents told me that the tornado was so wide, they "didn't know where to run."

One young man told me that he hid in a bathtub with a mattress over him. When the tornado passed, he crawled out of the tub to find that he was now outside, because his house had been blown away. He

Management Theories

Douglas McGregor, an American social psychologist, proposed his X and Y Theories in his 1960 book, *The Human Side of Enterprise*.

Theory X
(Task Oriented)

People dislike work, try to avoid it and must be forced and prodded. The belief is that people avoid responsibility and are motivated by the fear of punishment. Many managers lean toward this style of management, and often with poor results.

- Aloof
- Short-Tempered
- Results Driven
- Deadline Driven
- Intolerant
- Arrogant
- Distant
- Shouts
- Deadlines
- Ultimatums
- Demanding
- Poor Listener
- Does not Thank or Praise

Theory Y
(People Oriented)

Work is fulfilling to people and an environment should be created to facilitate growth and responsibility.

- The Manager Participates with Employees
- Interested in Growth and Development
- People Naturally Enjoy Work
- People Will Apply Self-Control and Self-Motivation
- Rewards Motivate—Fear Does Not
- People Enjoy Responsibility
- Imagination and Creativity is Common
- Praises and Thanks Good Performance
- Suggestions are Welcome

Theory Z
(Japanese Management Style)

Theory Z is not truly an extension of Theory X & Y, but emphasizes corporate loyalty, team-building, freedom and trust of the workers and a wholistic attitude. There is more focus on reliance of the worker, as opposed to Theories X & Y, which focus on the manager.

> From William Ouchi, in his 1981 book *Theory Z: How American Management Can Meet The Japanese Challenge*. William Ouchi is professor of management at UCLA.

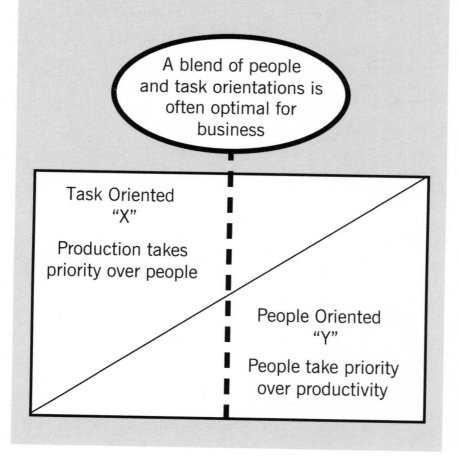

A blend of people and task orientations is often optimal for business

Task Oriented
"X"

Production takes priority over people

People Oriented
"Y"

People take priority over productivity

was lucky. Just down the street, the disaster blew apart nearly every house and caused twenty-seven deaths.

Unlike Tornado Alley—a high-risk strip from Illinois to Texas—the Jarrell situation was different. Prior to the Jarrell disaster, tornadoes were considered rare and, because the cost of storm cellar construction was significant, there wasn't a single storm cellar in the town.

Despite the fact that a tornado at Jarrell was considered rare, the fact remains that tornados *had* occurred there prior to the 1997 devastation. In 1987, for instance, a tornado destroyed many properties, including Doc's, a market and diner just a few miles from the Double Creek Subdivision.

After Mother Nature's 1997 visit, suspicions grew that the topography of Jarrell might be at special risk. Jarrell residents received gracious support from volunteers to rebuild, as well as help from insurance companies and governmental disaster relief funds. Fortunately, as they began to rebuild, the town residents learned their lesson. They took specific action by rebuilding their homes with concrete that would withstand tornado-strength winds. They also added a new feature to each home—a storm cellar.

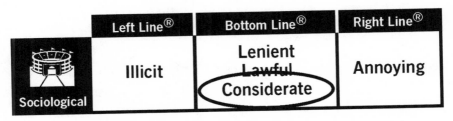

	Left Line®	Bottom Line®	Right Line®
Sociological	Illicit	Lenient ~~Lawful~~ **Considerate**	Annoying

Consideration Is Doing More Than the Rules Require

Once I was on a business trip in New York. As I often do, I had one of my children with me, and this time it was my son Michael. When we got into a taxi, Michael found a high-end "smart phone". We were trying to figure out who it belonged to when the phone rang. I answered it and on the other end was a frantic man looking for his lost phone.

I told him to meet my son outside of the New York convention center. A few minutes later, Michael came in and told me that the man had come to get his phone, and that he was so happy that he offered

Michael a hundred dollars. Michael loves money, but he turned down the cash. He knew that he was simply returning something to the rightful owner, and I was proud of that decision.

On another occasion, I was walking through a parking lot in Los Angeles with one of my business partners, Orell Anderson. All of a sudden, he stopped, took a quarter out of his pocket, and put it into a parking meter. I asked him why he had done this. He noticed that a meter maid was coming down the street and that someone had parked their car and the meter was expired; he didn't want them to get a ticket. He had no idea who owned the car, but he thought that he would help them out anyway.

I was impressed with his level of kindness and courtesy toward a person whom he had never met and whom he would likely never meet. But this is the kind of guy he is. He doesn't need any thanks or praise for it, he just likes to help others.

When there is no law that forces good behavior, good manners should fall into play. There were no laws stating that when the *Titanic* sank, gentlemen should put the women and children on the lifeboats first. While death was the certain and inevitable result of this action, and there was no law to force the men to do otherwise, this is what the majority of men did.

However, one man by the name of J. Bruce Ismay, the managing director of White Star—the company that owned the *Titanic*—shoved his way onto a lifeboat. For the rest of his life, he was severely criticized for leaving his ship while more than 1,500 other people were left to die. He had not broken any laws, but he certainly displayed bad behavior.

He was not alone. Another first-class passenger, William Carter, was on the same lifeboat. Carter later testified that he had placed his wife and children on another lifeboat before getting onto one himself. It was determined, however, that his wife and children were on a lifeboat that had been launched fifteen minutes *later*. Mrs. Carter sued for divorce.

In our personal lives, we all have basic roles and responsibilities, but to enjoy more-than-average achievement, we must do more than just what the basic rules require.

The Four Key
Organizational Roles & Responsibilities

Organizational Development: What do we do to keep existing clients, customers, or members happy, while continually developing new growth?

Project Management: How efficiently do we manage a task or project?

People Development: How well do we treat others in the organization and contribute to their training and development?

Technical Skills: How proficient are we at what we do? Are we on the leading edge with our technical knowledge?

My roles include being a husband, a parent, a member of a church, and a member of various clubs and community organizations. In business, I have the role of being the CEO of a consulting firm, an instructor, and a member of two professional organizations.

In our personal lives, we are well-served to ask ourselves the question, "Are my roles defined and my responsibilities met?"

Dr. Martin Luther King, Jr., said, "If a man is called to be a street sweeper, he should sweep the streets even as Michelangelo painted, or as Beethoven composed music, or as Shakespeare wrote poetry. He should sweep streets so well that all the hosts of heaven and earth will pause to say, *here lives a great street sweeper who did his job well.*"

Doing More Than Expected, and Enjoying It

On one of my frequent business trips, I was reading a book about my roles and responsibilities in raising my children. As I was reading, I became increasingly concerned that there was no way I'd remember all the information. I realized, though, that there was one simple theme to the book: spend time with my kids.

I have always felt that my basic duties demanded that I support my family, but I wanted to do more than just my basic duties. The Dalai Lama says, "A loving atmosphere in your home is the foundation for your life." David O. McKay was a little more direct when he said, "No other success can compensate for failure in the home."

At that point, I decided to do two things:

First, I committed to frequently take one of my kids out to lunch or dinner. This would give us a chance for good old one-on-one time.

I thought this would be a good thing, but I had no idea just how great an idea this was. When I go to their elementary school to pick my children up, they're just bursting at the seams to see me. They tell all their friends that they're going out to lunch with their dad. The whole class stares as I pick them up. I get to meet a lot of their friends, so now I have faces to put with the names that I hear about at dinner. At times, they tell me everything, and we talk about things that I think

Effort-Talent Model

In an organization, effort should be made to always motivate upward, in combination with training and development to increase the level of talent. Steady supporters are of great value to an organization, but "dead weight" can be a drain.

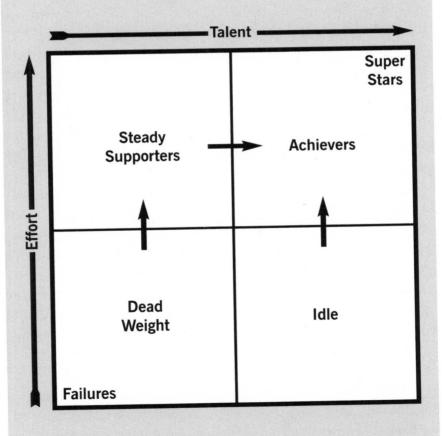

many kids would not discuss with their parents. Other times, we don't talk about much. There is no agenda, except to hang out together.

They know that I really love them, not just by my telling them, but by taking a little time to step out of my "expected" role.

Second, I decided to take one of my kids on business trips whenever possible. I realized that I can fly myself and one of my kids in coach for the price of one first-class ticket.

On my first "accompanied" business trip, I took my oldest son, Michael, to New Mexico where I was doing research at the National Atomic Museum.

We met General Paul Tibbets, who flew the Enola Gay and dropped the first atomic bomb on Hiroshima. I'm sure that my eight-year-old son had no idea of the legend that he had met and visited with, but it was a trip that neither he nor I will forget.

Michael asked him if he had been scared when he dropped the bomb, and General Tibbets quickly told my son, "No!" He explained that he had spent so much time in preparation, that there was nothing to fear, which was a good lesson for both of us.

When Michael asked him what it was like when he dropped the bomb, General Tibbets told him that the bomb blast shook the plane, and it felt like he got a "good spanking."

Then, my son asked the question we all wonder about, but only an eight-year-old boy would have the guts to ask: "Do you have any regret about dropping the bomb?" Tibbets's answer was immediate, self-confident, and direct. He had seen the movies of the horrific actions of the Japanese soldiers, he had seen many friends lose their lives defending against these aggressors who resorted to kamikaze tactics, and he was convinced that the war would go on for years without this action. America was not the aggressor, but was defending against one. No, he had no regrets about dropping "the bomb."

This was a priceless educational experience.

On my next business trip, I took my seven-year-old son, Steve, to San Antonio. After a day on the plane, in rental cars, and getting lost, we finally sat down at a restaurant near our hotel. To me, it was just another business trip. When we got to the restaurant, I asked Steven what the best day in his life had been. I expected him to tell me about a particularly "profitable" Christmas or birthday, but I nearly fell off my seat when he told me that it was "today." While it was just another trip for me, for this little guy it had been an incredible adventure to go on a business trip with his dad.

Realizing that this was so important to my son, I changed my outlook and focused on ensuring that this would be a great trip for Steve. We went to the hotel and got every pamphlet about every available tour and place of interest. We took a ghost-hunting tour, visited the Alamo, took a river boat ride, went to Ripley's Believe It or Not (where Steve saw the real shrunken head he still talks about), saw two I-Max movies, and ate lots of Texan food.

On my third trip, I took my daughter, Britten, to San Francisco. She was just four years old. She almost came out of her skin with excitement over her trip. My wife, Melanie, had packed Britten's Barbie backpack with all kinds of treats and a little camera. People stopped to watch my little girl in the airport with her Barbie roll-along suitcase. After my meetings, we walked around Fisherman's Wharf, played in the sand and ate ice cream. She still talks about going down the "crooked road," Lombard Street.

Since these trips, there have been many others. I realize in business that I have a responsibility to my clients and that on some trips it wouldn't be appropriate to bring my children. I've had so much fun with them, though, that I now put a clause into my consulting contract. Either I fly first class by myself or, at my discretion, I can bring a family member. I once had a prospective client cross that clause out of the proposal, and I promptly "fired him." I will only associate with clients who respect my position on this matter.

While I study disasters as a career, the biggest disaster to me would be to fall short of my responsibilities to my family.

Sociological Insights

- We all have roles and responsibilities, which should be carefully defined.
- Roles and responsibilities can be defined for both personal and business life.
- Everyone we deal with should have clear and defined responsibilities. Vague responsibilities only lead to confusion and frustration.
- A promise should never be made that cannot be kept.
- Being negligent in our responsibilities is on a par with being a coward in the hour of danger.
- Sometimes meeting our responsibility means just spending some time with people.
- "Management by wondering" can be very effective.
- If we are fully prepared, we have nothing to fear.
- The ideal decision will create a benefit for ourselves, others, and society in general.
- Once we have defined our competition, we must build barriers against them.
- Only our competition should be damaged by the decisions that we make.
- The best people in business are team players.
- Achievers do not necessarily feel superior to anyone, but they certainly do not feel inferior to anyone either.

Chapter Four

Influential
Get the Word Out

"**C**ommunication" means far more than merely having words come out of our mouths, or writing letters or memos. Everyday, many such "communications" are regularly ignored or just quickly forgotten. True influence occurs when our message grabs attention and then impacts both sides of the recipient's brains, meaning that it both makes sense and hits an emotional nerve. As a result, action is taken.

There are basically four ways to communicate. These are: our personal example, one-on-one, presentations to a group, or a written document.

Communication through example is the quintessential way to send a message. Actions have always spoken louder than words, and example is far louder than anything one could ever say. This is why celebrity endorsements are so effective. Seeing a familiar person actually using a product or service has a big impact.

With one-on-one communication, it is always critical to control what comes out of our mouths. It is important that we "take the temperature" before saying anything. When speaking to a group, the preparation period is important for delivering a message on target. For every minute of a group presentation, we must spend at least five minutes preparing, and often far more. When speaking, we must choose our words carefully, capture attention, and implant the message into other's thoughts and emotions. In other words, the most effective message is one where our message is both logical and thoughtful and, above all, is actually applied in our own lives. As a result, a desired objective is obtained.

In getting the word out, relationships are essential. Aligning one's self with those with a similar vision creates a synergy that enables one to achieve far more than they could have on their own. These relationships apply in both personal and business life. Ray Kroc, the founder of McDonald's, once said, "You're only as good as the people you hire."

Parents tell their kids to pick "good friends" and we all want to work with "good people." Good people seek common ground, are quick to avoid or resolve conflict, respect others' points of view and generally enjoy helping others as well as seeing others succeed. On the other hand, toxic people are those who perpetuate conflict and enjoy seeing others fail.

A key to achievement is determining who and who not to align oneself with. After all, family and friends are the best measure of success.

Bad Manners Send an *Insensitive* Message

When I founded and directed a group in a large consulting firm, I hired some of the brightest minds in the field. Their poor table manners with clients, however, were really a problem.

One guy would sit and lick his spoon like a lollipop. Then he would eat using his fork like a lever as he rotated his plate around. I asked him why he did this and he told me, true to his engineering background, that it was a more efficient form of eating. Two guys would smear their entire piece of bread with butter and prop it up in their hands throughout the entire lunch so they could take a bite anytime. Still another would eat pseudo-European style, so that he would not have to trade hands with his utensils and thus could plow through his lunch more quickly. Elbows on the table were standard.

When it came to a technical problem, they were the best, but when it came to good manners, it was almost comical . . . except the clients weren't laughing.

One client confided in me that he passed over using one of my guys because he was concerned, not with his professional qualifications or intelligence but that his manners might come off poorly in front of others. Now the situation had gone from being an annoyance to costing us business. Their insensitivity had become a Left Line problem. It was my little in-house etiquette disaster, and I had to do something.

After thinking about it, I decided to have a "boot camp" day where we would discuss a variety of administrative and technical issues. During lunch, I hired a "Miss Manners" to address the group on the topic of business and dining etiquette. I had a long conversation with her, telling her about the behavior that was causing the embarrassment.

The session went pretty well, but when Miss Manners wasn't looking, one of the guys would make faces. Not surprisingly, he was the worst offender. After being instructed on the fundamentals of dining etiquette, we all ate lunch while Miss Manners watched us and took notes. Most of the group got the message and did well, but of course there were slip-ups. Her name was Diana, so we decided that if any of us were violating any of the rules of manners in front of a client, we could tip off our colleague by saying, "Oh by the way, Diana called." If the offense was really out of bounds, we would say, "Diana called, and she said it was an emergency!"

It was not a matter of "acting superior" to anyone. Good etiquette is showing the other party that you respect him or her enough to behave appropriately.

For Better or Worse, the First Impression Is the Lasting One

The *Exxon Valdez* spill was not a particularly large one. It didn't even rank as one of the world's top ten, but it's probably the most well known.

At 12:04 AM, on March 24, 1989, an oil tanker loaded with 1.2 million barrels of North Slope crude oil, ran aground on Bligh Reef in the northeastern portion of Prince William Sound, Alaska. Approximately one-fifth of the cargo—11.2 million gallons—spilled into the ocean.

Oddly enough, the delay in responding was due to the fact that, two months earlier, Exxon had closed down its Emergency Response Division, citing cost and viability issues. Containment efforts were eventually started in a couple of days but, after three days of calm seas,

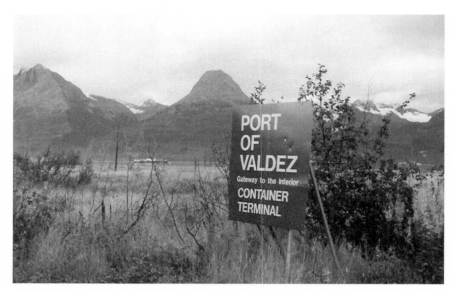

The Valdez oil tanker took on its load here at the Port of Valdez. The town of Valdez actually never had a drop of oil on its shores.

strong northeasterly winds arose and dispersed the oil beyond any hope of containment. As a result, the clean-up efforts took three years, and involved more than 11,000 people and 1,400 marine vessels. On June 10, 1992, the federal government issued a letter officially stating that the cleanup effort was concluded. It had cost $2.1 billion.

While much of the public is oblivious to this, Exxon did an outstanding job in cleaning up the spill. Nonetheless, their initial stall those first two days left a negative image that the media fed on for months. To this day, Exxon still operates under that stigma.

Constructive Criticism Can Work

A number of experts tried to come to Exxon's aid in those first few hours, but Exxon wasn't listening. Yet, listening to others' suggestions and criticisms can be extremely helpful. Norman Vincent Peale said, "The trouble with most of us is that we would rather be ruined by praise than saved by criticism."

When I wrote a technical textbook on measuring the economic impacts of disasters, *Real Estate Damages*, I knew I was pioneering new territory. This was the first book in history on the topic, and I had no beaten path or mentor to follow. When I completed the first draft, I sent it out and invited criticism. And I got it . . . lots of it! Looking back, the book in its first-draft form would have been a disaster. But by listening to the criticism and making several changes, the book was a success.

We need to invite honest feedback, then act on it. At the same time, we are not doing anyone a favor when we sugarcoat our criticism and critiques. As Benjamin Franklin said, "Love your enemies, for they tell you your faults."

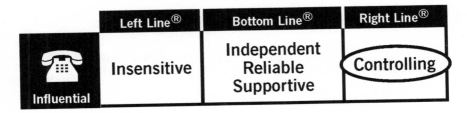

Extreme *Control* Causes Extreme Damage

In a classic display of Right Line control, on August 9, 1969, the followers of Charles Manson murdered actress Sharon Tate, her unborn child, and others. These were some of the most heinous crimes in history, and the world watched intently as Manson and his followers were convicted of the crimes.

Certainly, one of the most intriguing facts in this case is the fact that Manson was convicted of murder, even though he physically did not commit the murders and was not even at the crime scene. His influence was so controlling that he had the ability to have others commit murder on his behalf. His control techniques were very slow and incremental, while, at the same time, entirely effective.

While Manson deployed the most extreme type of control, common "control freaks" can cause long-term damage in both the people and situations they abuse.

In more everyday matters, when one exhibits too much control over another, it sends a message that, "I'm not confident in your abilities" or even worse, "I don't really trust you."

A 10,000 square foot Mediterranean mansion now sits on the site of the Sharon Tate crime scene in Los Angeles.

Theodore Roosevelt said, "The best executive is the one who has the sense enough to pick the good men to do what he wants done, and self-restraint enough to keep from meddling with them while they do it." Many other great thinkers have commented on the need to respect others' independence.

Abraham Lincoln said, "You cannot help men permanently by doing for them what they could and should do for themselves."

Andrew Carnegie put it this way: "There is no use whatever trying to help people who do not help themselves. You cannot push anyone up a ladder unless he is willing to climb himself."

And Harry Truman said, "The best way to give advice to your children is to find out what they want and then advise them to do it."

An *Independent* Thinker Knows "When to Put a Cork in It"

One common trait among the genuinely powerful is the ability to be silent. As the old saying goes, "We have two ears, but only one mouth."

I was once driving around Chicago with a man who called himself "a little Polish guy" whose father had constantly told him that "You can't learn anything when your mouth is moving . . . so stick a cork in it!" I had a good laugh over this comment, but there is a great deal of truth to it. I've had the opportunity to train new consultants who are coming right out of college. I've taken them to various meetings where I instruct them to just listen. Despite this instruction, many of them can't resist the temptation to speak up at every opportunity. They invariably come off looking just a little too eager and sometimes even foolish.

> *When George Washington presided over the delegation that wrote the Declaration of Independence, he could have had a virtual monopoly over the proceedings. Instead, he spoke only once, and that was to basically comment that enough had been done and it was time to wrap it up.*

Charles de Gaulle observed that, "Silence is the ultimate weapon of power. Remember to never miss a great opportunity to shut up."

The Independent Also Know When It's Time to Speak Up

My son has a young friend we call "Michael Z," who plays soccer. During one game, the star player was expelled for two games for unsportsmanlike behavior, so the coach had this same player suit up in another kid's uniform to play the next game.

The entire team was uncomfortable with the coach's cheating, but only Michael Z had the courage and independence to speak up and say something. Once he did, the whole team backed Michael Z, and the coach backed down. That was pretty impressive behavior from a ten-year-old.

Reliability Makes All the Difference in the World

It is common that, when reacting to some type of tragedy such as a fire or earthquake, the first items most people grab are pictures of family and friends. Indeed, these relationships are the most valuable things we have in life because they're people we've come to rely on and vice versa. In business, the same applies—one's contacts and relationships are incredibly valuable.

The old saying my parents told me was that "the best way to have a friend is to be a friend."

Dale Carnegie said, "You can make more friends in two months by becoming interested in other people than you can in two years by trying to get other people interested in you."

Albert Schweitzer added, "Do something for somebody every day for which you do not get paid."

When I think of "unconscious reliability"—that is, acting reliably without thought to plotting one's just reward—I'm often reminded of the old story where a grandfather and grandson are walking along the beach. As they walked, the grandfather would pause every time he saw a sand dollar, pick it up and throw it into the sea. His grandson asked why he did this, and the grandfather replied that if the sand dollar were not in the water, it would dry out and die. The young boy said that this did not seem so smart to him, because with so many sand dollars, it would be impossible to make any real difference. The grandfather picked up another sand dollar, threw it into the sea and then said, "Well, it will make all the difference in the world to that one."

Associations Speak Volumes

It is important that we consciously make decisions about the people we associate with. As George Washington said, "Associate yourself with men of good quality if you esteem your own reputation, for 'tis better to be alone than in bad company."

I directed a practice in a large consulting firm, but when the firm merged, I was expected to integrate my practice with a similar group in the other firm. At that point, I was in my own "association" quandary, as the leader of that practice had been associated with Charles Keating and his massive real estate frauds. Upon learning this and other information, I left the firm. It was a decision I never regretted.

It is just as important to know who not to associate with as it is with whom to associate.

Simple *Supportive* Habits Have a Big Impact

Durham Woods is a thousand-unit apartment complex located in Edison, New Jersey. Near midnight, on March 23, 1994, an underground, high-pressure, methane gas pipeline exploded near the complex. The explosion created a crater sixty feet deep and sent a three-hundred-foot fireball into the air that could be seen by residents of New Jersey, New York, and Pennsylvania. The event was so disastrous that it was designated a federal disaster area.

While the fire burned out of control, it took workers nearly three hours to turn off the gas flow, which they eventually did by turning a valve one small turn at a time. The apartment's 1,500 tenants were forced to flee their homes in the middle of the night. A total of 128 apartments were completely destroyed. The next morning, a team of police officers conducted the grim task of searching for bodies.

When I consulted on this case, I toured the area that had been incinerated.

The fire had burned so hot that it literally melted the red lights on the fire trucks and charred trees that were hundred of yards away.

Pipeline corridors like this one at Durham Woods run for thousands of miles throughout the United States.

Cars that had been parked in the apartment's parking lot had melted into liquid pools of metal.

The apartment buildings themselves were burned right down to their foundations, and no framing remained. I could not help but ask the owners of the development how many people had died. I was happy—and somewhat surprised—to learn that *nobody had died.* Even though the tragedy occurred near midnight, all of the 1,500 victims successfully escaped.

How could this have been possible? The answer was simple. The neighborhood was full of people who had developed solid, supportive relationships with each other. When the explosion woke up some people, they took the time to bang on doors to wake up all their neighbors before fleeing for their lives. Certainly, without this reaction, dozens or even hundreds of people would have been killed. *These strong friendships literally saved lives.*

Mother Teresa offered some advice about relationships: "The biggest disease today is not leprosy or tuberculosis, but rather the feeling of being unwanted." While some may think her comment

This playground at the Durham Woods Apartments sits near the epicenter of the pipeline explosion. Note how the trees in the background are singed black from the fireball.

applies only to those living in poverty, this observation applies across the board . . . at family kitchen tables, in neighborhood communities, in school classrooms, and in any workplace.

Better organizations will go out of their way to express appreciation. This can be accomplished in a number of ways, such as awards dinners, votes for the "employee of the month," surprise gifts or trips. Simple gestures like the old pat on the back or simply saying "thank you" are essential.

Plain old basic courtesy would be a big step in the right direction, too. I once observed an attorney who had an outstanding legal secretary. She was sharp, well dressed, very professional, and pleasant and was incredibly skilled at keeping all of his documents organized. When he asked for something, she would find it and hand it to him in seconds but, in all the times I observed, he never said, "Thanks."

Eventually, she quit. He was stunned because he paid her a great salary. He didn't realize that it isn't just money that brings satisfaction from a job. Simple courtesy would have preserved an otherwise great business relationship.

Simple gestures can go a long way. Thank you cards, notes, clipping and sending an article that may be of interest to someone, a quick e-mail or phone call can mean the world to someone.

Being Supportive Does Not Mean Caving In

One of my family rules for skiing is that any whining or complaining is simply not allowed. I will help anyone who has a good attitude and is trying their best, but I will not let any complaining interfere with the family's fun. My son Michael knew how to ski, but on the first run of the day he fell down and started to whine and complain loudly. I went up to help him, but I also reminded him of the rule. He chose, instead, to continue to complain, so I told him I would check on his attitude on my next run.

I skied off with my son Steven. On the next run, Michael was still sitting there in the snow. I asked him about his attitude and he still whined, so I took off again. On my third run, he'd gotten the message. I asked him how he was doing, and he knew that I meant business. He replied with a big smile that he was doing great. I helped him up, and he skied beautifully the rest of the day. I knew that he could do it, and I knew he could have a good attitude if he just changed his mind about it. I set the rules and enforced them. I know that if I had given in, I would have spent the day with a little boy who complained the whole time. By being supportive and still making him responsible for his behavior, we both had a great day.

Pass Along the Lessons

My wife, Melanie, has a great influence on my kids, and she always makes them a top priority before her own interests. Her decorating skills make Martha Stewart look bland, and she will spend literally months planning for one of the kids' birthday parties. At first, I didn't get why she would go to such extreme efforts, but looking back at the photos and videos, our children now have an appreciation for her love and her wonderful influence.

I've been influenced by my observations, and now teach these fourteen lessons to my children:

1. *When a problem arises, keep it in perspective*. Don't let a little problem wreck a good friendship or business relationship. A little time may cure it. Remember, as Mahatma Gandhi said, "Honest differences are often a healthy sign of progress."

2. *Learn to apologize and learn to forgive.*

3. *Laugh at yourself.*

4. *Always live the golden rule*. "The best way to make a friend is to be a friend," and, as Abraham Lincoln said, "The best way to destroy an enemy is to turn him into a friend."

5. It is important to be kind to everyone, but it is important to *make good friends who share the same values*.

6. *It is better to have one or two genuine friends than two hundred superficial ones.*

7. *Express your gratitude and display your respect* in the form of good etiquette.

8. *Listen to others.* The Dalai Lama said, "Remember that silence is sometimes the best answer."

9. *Be quick to compliment and slow to criticize.* To paraphrase Dale Carnegie, You'll make more friends being interested in other people than you will by getting other people interested in you.

10. *Never forget the people who support you.* Walt Disney said, "It seems to me shallow and arrogant for any man in these times to claim he is completely self-made, that he owes all his success to his own unaided efforts. Many hands and hearts and minds contribute to anyone's notable achievements."

11. *Don't let the underachievers drag you down.* In order to be "outstanding," one must "stand out," and anyone who stands out is automatically going to be a target for criticism from underachievers. Don't waste your energy trying to please these types of people.

12. *Never continue in a relationship where others fail to respect you*, or are abusive in any way. Whether in our own individual lives or in business working with others, we should always ask ourselves, "Do I really practice listening to others?" and "Is my voice being heard?"

13. *We are all in "sales."* At times, being supportive means being persuasive. In this respect, we are all in the business of sales. We all have customers, or people to whom we report or must please in some way. These "customers" could be bosses, clients, students, friends, spouses, or children. "Sales" could mean pastries at a bakery, a car at the dealership, a proposal for a client, a job application, a college application, or motivating a child to study harder. The Left Line person feels he is above "selling," while a reliable person is proficient at presenting his ideas one-on-one, in front of a group or in a written statement or report.

14. *"Example" is the most persuasive trait of all.* Albert Schweitzer said, "Example is not the main thing influencing others. It is the only thing." When it comes to key relationships, our behavior is like an echo . . . what we send out is largely what we get back.

Influential Insights

- Family and friends are our best indication of worth.
- Our key assets are our relationships, which should be treated like the valuable assets that they are.
- Do something for someone every day for which you do not get paid.
- Associate with good people. It's better to be alone than in bad company.
- Many people can handle adversity, but only the strong can handle success.
- Avoid getting a big head. Cemeteries are filled with "indispensable" men.
- Silence can be a powerful trait.
- People will inevitably support ideas when they have input and authorship.
- Good leaders know when to back off.
- Example is far more important than words.
- Invite criticism. Our enemies will show us where our flaws are.
- Bumps and bruises are inevitable on any journey. Don't let little things injure a great relationship.
- "Good manners" are not a matter of acting superior, but rather showing respect for others.
- A person's name is music to his or her own ears.
- Basic courtesy is not an option. It is critical to success.
- Relationships that are not actively built up will deteriorate.
- A bad example can be as valuable a lesson as a good one.
- Being outstanding inherently means that someone must stand out. And "standing out" will inevitably invite criticism. Deal with it.
- Customers and clients are rarely stupid. It is futile to argue with a person that is bright, intelligent, and always right.

Part III

Productivity

Productivity is based in the Latin *pro*, meaning "forward" or "in favor of," and *ductus* meaning "to lead." It is a social principle meaning "fit for production" or to "lead or bring forth" and to "create" something strong and of social worth and *valoir* or "value." Without productivity, there is no value. "Productivity" includes a combination of "Environmental," "Financial," and "Physical" issues.

Chapter Five

Physical
Keep in Shape!

Originally stated by the German scientist Rudolf Clausius, *The Second Law of Thermodynamics*, can be paraphrased as,

Anything in the physical world not acted upon will eventually result in entropy or decay.

In other words, our physical health, as well as our products and services, will all go to shambles if we don't continuously intervene and act upon them.

This is a critical scientific observation. Everything else becomes irrelevant if one's physical condition is shot. Good health and pumping up our heart and muscles several times a week is just basic. Likewise, every business becomes irrelevant if the products or services are not fit for the market. It is essential to monitor consumer and clients' needs, and continually pump up the quality of our products and services.

If we are not actively maintaining and improving the physical things in life, then the forces of nature will tear them down. This is simply the laws of physics. Acceptance of this principle is crucial to remaining relevant.

An *Apathetic* Organization Might as Well Close Its Doors Now . . . Because That's Where It's Headed

Several years ago, I bought a Mercedes. I didn't just buy *any* Mercedes—I bought the top-of-the-line model from an "authorized" dealer. But this thing was a lemon.

I took it to the dealer and was amazed at their apathetic re-sponse. My car was consuming large amounts of oil and blowing massive amounts of white smoke out the exhaust, but the dealer wouldn't do anything about it, even though the car was under war-ranty. I took the car in several times and wrote letter after letter, but nothing happened. I hired an attorney and even tried to force the dealership to honor its warranty. Despite obvious and glaring evi-dence that the car had serious problems, the dealer's attorney did nothing. I really could *not* believe it.

Finally, I tried something that I should have done a lot earlier: I called the national headquarters of Mercedes. They immediately directed me to another dealer, which promptly diagnosed a serious valve problem and repaired it at no cost.

While I was happy that my problem had finally been resolved, I was obviously unhappy about the first dealer's behavior. As a result, and on at least seven occasions, I've steered friends and colleagues away from the apathetic dealer to the one, instead, that helped me. This action may not ruin the bad dealer, but I've diverted several hun-dreds of thousands of dollars away from the apathetic dealer.

Excessive Behavior Is Also "Out of Bounds"

The Rolls Royce has a metal body that is handcrafted for every car. Its leather interior is hand stitched. While Rolls Royce is a gor-geous automobile, it's not as commercially successful in terms of gross revenues as Toyota or Nissan. Jaguar, Mercedes, and BMW were all once considered exceptionally well-crafted foreign automobiles, but over time it became apparent that this emphasis was not the most profitable path to take. Not enough of the automobile market is will-ing to pay for excessive Right Line features. These manufacturers made serious cutbacks and now offer lower-end cars that compete with the automobile mainstream. While they have lost some prestige in the process, the shift has kept them viable.

In the consulting business, the "product" that rolls through the "assembly line" is the research. If you're apathetic toward research and development, you'll lose the interest of your market completely. Going overboard to an excessive side, however, can be just as alienating.

Once I was working on a project that involved a large-scale oil spill. A researcher I hired was responsible for locating similar oil spills and finding out the details. After a while, he reported back with twenty-seven case studies and he had voluminous amounts of data on each one. The quantity of information was overwhelming; it was simply overkill. I really only needed the best five or six case studies. Together, we selected the best data and put the rest aside.

We all know people who end up on a path of excess, such as eating at fast-food restaurants daily, working eighteen-hour days or athletically training six hours a day, seven days a week. Even nature has a way of forcing excessive Right Line people to back off through joint and tendon injuries, adult diabetes, strokes, and even nervous breakdowns.

> *Excessive action may initially take us farther, but if unchecked, we will inevitably break down.*

Relaxation Is Actually a Major Ingredient of Success

When I turned forty, I went in for my annual checkup. While I thought this would be another routine exam, my doctor sat down and had a talk with me that I'll never forget. He told me about stress and how serious the effects are. Stress causes an entire stream of medical problems. He told me that, from that point on, I needed to take a two-week vacation every year.

Until that time, my vacations were three-day weekends or, at most, a week in Hawaii. Throughout my trip, I'd have my cell phone and laptop fired up and going. My kids would wonder why I was in the hotel room while they were in the pool or at the beach. When I got back from my "vacation," I was exhausted and, like I hear many colleagues say, I needed a vacation from my vacation.

My doctor told me that one week's vacation wasn't enough, because that first week simply allows the body to wind down. The second week is where the body truly gets some rest. Further, he defined a vacation as time away from e-mails, cell phones, and business of any kind. He told me to take some time every year and just back off and *relax*.

Stress Management

  Impacts of Stress

Competition	Deadlines	Death	Disappointments
Divorce	Financial Problems	Losing a Job	Marriage
New Child	New Job	New Life Style	New School
Noise	Overload	People Conflicts	Poor Environment

Mental

irritable, scared, anxious, moody, fears, forgetfulness, low self-esteem, preoccupation, low concentration, worry

Behavioral

crying, drugs, alcohol, smoking, eating disorders, impulsiveness, accident prone

Physical

perspiration, trembling, heart rate, indigestion, tiredness, headaches, sleeping problems, backaches, illness

 Stress Management

Stress has (1) a source, and (2) an effect. For example, if a poor personal relationship causes stress, one can (1) address the source (the relationship problem itself), (2) manage the effects of the stress, or both.

In some circumstances, the cause of stress cannot be controlled (e.g., the death of a loved one) so stress management is the only alternative. These techniques include imagery, meditation, music, physical relaxation, and yoga.

Physical exercise is an outstanding stress-reduction technique. It not only reduces stress, but also relaxes muscles, improves sleep, improves blood flow, flushes out toxins, and releases into your blood stream endorphins, which are chemicals that bring feelings of happiness and a sense of well-being. Always talk to your doctor prior to starting an exercise program.

Stress Management

Relaxation Response by Dr. Herbert Benson

- Sit quietly in a comfortable position.
- Close your eyes.
- Deeply relax all of your muscles, from your toes up to your nose.
- Breathe through your nose. Become aware of your breathing. As you exhale, say the word, "ONE", silently to yourself. For example: breathe IN...OUT, "ONE", IN...OUT, "ONE", etc. Breathe easily and naturally.
- Continue for 10 to 20 minutes. You may open your eyes to check the time, but do not use an alarm. When you finish, sit quietly for several minutes, at first with your eyes closed, then with your eyes opened. Do not stand up for a few minutes.
- Do not worry about whether or not you achieve a deep state of relaxation. When distracted, simply return to repeating "ONE."

I took his advice and embarked on a two-week road trip with my family. We drove up through Yellowstone and out to Wyoming. We saw a rodeo, lots of wildlife, went horseback riding, did some fishing, and, basically, got away from it all. When I returned to the office, I was fully rested and ready to go. This had been great advice from my doctor.

Even Olympic Athletes Have to Back Off

Peter Vidmar was the team captain for the United States Gymnastics Team at the 1984 Olympics. He's won two gold metals and one silver medal, including one for scoring a perfect "10" for his pommel horse routine. He was later inducted into the Olympic Hall of Fame as one of the nation's top one hundred Olympians.

One can only imagine the amount of dedication Peter must have had to accomplish such an impressive feat, and yet he told me an interesting story about how his coaches wanted him to practice every day, but he refused. Peter practiced intensely six days a week, but he insisted on resting on Sundays. At first, his coach was disappointed,

Large cracks that were caused by the earthquake are still visible today.

but then it became apparent that Peter's performance was not suffering at all. In fact, he excelled.

Backing off and relaxing is a critical element of even peak, Olympic- level achievement.

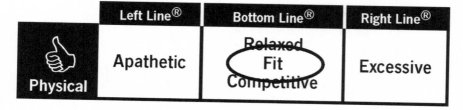

	Left Line®	Bottom Line®	Right Line®
👍 Physical	Apathetic	~~Relaxed~~ Fit ~~Competitive~~	Excessive

Peter recently told me that sports doctors have discovered that the body's performance goes in cycles, and is capable of peak Olympic performance only a couple times a year. Even Olympians know that they cannot be "on" all the time and have to back off periodically.

Are You *Fit* Enough to Hang On?

A few years ago, a TV documentary about people who had survived disaster caught my attention. In one instance, a woman was

The Great Alaskan Earthquake was so violent that entire continental plates heaved up and down more than twelve feet. This house once sat above sea level, but after the quake, it sits below sea level and has been destroyed by the tides.

featured who, as a young girl, had survived the tidal waves resulting from the 1964 Alaskan earthquake.

I was interested in studying the event, so I called the only person I knew from Alaska, Steve McSwain. Steve and I had initially met at a conference in Washington, D.C., and he was helpful in showing me around Alaska. At the end of our afternoon together, Steve said, "Hey Randy, you need to meet my wife. When she was a little girl she was hit by the tidal waves of the Great Alaska Earthquake!" It was an amazing coincidence, but Steve's wife was the woman I had watched on TV who prompted me to go to Alaska in the first place.

I met Linda, and she recounted her incredible story as we all drove from Anchorage to Seward to survey the tidal wave sites. After the earthquake, tidal waves came up to her home and began pounding away at the foundation. Her father took the family upstairs, but soon the tidal waves got larger, and they had to climb onto the roof for safety. For the entire cold Alaskan night, her father overcame intense physical strain and literally *held onto his family* as their house was pounded off the foundation and into trees and other structures. Even my "weekend warrior" buddies would have difficulty meeting that kind of physical demand.

The entire family was put onto the presumed dead list and the surviving townspeople were amazed when her family walked into town the next day. Certainly Linda's father was a bona fide hero for keeping his family together on the roof all through the night.

An interesting issue comes from this disaster. In any threatening situation, most parents would go to any physical extreme to protect their children.

The question is, "Are you also willing to take the heroic step of getting involved in the more mundane issue of routine health and fitness?"

Obviously, if we don't take care of ourselves, we may not even be around to take care of our children, crisis or not.

Using the Focus Factor, it is easy to see the attributes of one who has a "body of failure." This individual has a compulsive mindset, where the "sweet satisfaction" of eating a tempting treat wins out over the other costs and benefits. Conversely, the "balanced mindset" sees all the issues clearly and acts accordingly.

No amount of knowledge, learning, philosophies, or intention makes any difference in this bottom line:

One can have considerable knowledge about exercising; he or she can have a firm faith and belief that it works and can even own the finest gym equipment available . . . but the waistline only responds to action.

Discipline and action are the absolute requirements for physical fitness. There are no substitutes.

I was a skinny kid. In high school, I worked in a pizza parlor and could eat three pizzas and still lose ten pounds. That trait continued into my twenties. When I turned thirty, I found a new stomach appearing that was a little disturbing but, with a little effort, it would go away. By forty, the party was clearly over. If I even *looked* at a pizza, I would gain ten pounds.

Eat Right & Exercise

Eat Right

Yes   No

Enjoy good fresh foods   Avoid or strictly limit.

Yes	No
Fish	Sugar
Chicken	High-Fructose
Salads	Refined Carbs
Fruit	Pasta
Vegetables	Whole Wheat*
Egg Whites	Multi-Grain*
Cheese	Red Meats
Whole Grains	Fried Foods
Complex Carbs	Caffeine
Water	Alcohol

* These sound healthy, but are actually processed flour. Whole grain is best.

Always consult with your doctor regarding diet and exercise issues.

Exercise

This table gives approximate calories spent per hour by a 100-, 150- and 200- pound person doing a particular activity.

Activity	100 lb	150 lb	200 lb
Bike, 6 mph	160	240	312
Bike, 12 mph	270	410	534
Jog, 7 mph	610	920	1,230
Jump Rope	500	750	1,000
Run, 5.5 mph	440	660	962
Run, 10 mph	850	1,280	1,664
Swim, 25 yds/min	185	275	358
Swim, 50 yds/min	325	500	650
Tennis Singles	265	400	535
Walk, 2 mph	160	240	312
Walk, 3 mph	210	320	416
Walk, 4.5 mph	295	440	572

Source: American Heart Association

Drink Water

✓ The human body is more than 70% water.

✓ Many Americans are chronically dehydrated.

✓ The thirst mechanism is often mistaken for hunger.

✓ One glass of water can shut down hunger pangs.

✓ Dehydration slows down one's metabolism.

✓ Lack of water triggers daytime fatigue.

✓ Dehydration can trigger fuzzy memory, trouble with reading & basic math, and joint pains.

✓ 8 X 8 Rule: Eight, eight ounce glasses, or for adults 2.5 liters/day.

Eating Healthy

As the Focus Factor™ demonstrates, fitness is a matter of seeing both the long- and short-term costs and benefits clearly. The unbalanced mindset sees only the immediate "benefit" of overeating, while the balanced mindset sees the whole picture clearly.

FOCUS FACTOR
Unbalanced Mindset

	Cost	Benefit
Long-Term	Time Discipline	High Energy Appearance Clothes Fit Longer Life
Immediate	Bloated Feeling Tired Uncomfortable	**Sweet Satisfaction**

FOCUS FACTOR
Balanced Mindset

	Cost	Benefit
Long-Term	Time Discipline	High Energy Appearance Clothes Fit Longer Life
Immediate	Bloated Feeling Tired Uncomfortable	Sweet Satisfaction

While being overweight seemed to be an absolute impossibility when I was younger, it was a now a problem I was forced to deal with. Initially, I became like many people and exercised regularly every few months, then dropped the regimen in favor of long and sedentary periods of guilt.

On one occasion, I spoke with a man who was financially success-ful as a top executive in a large company. I asked him if there were anything he would do differently, given from all the experience he had gained. I expected that his answer might be about some business opportunity he had missed, or a trip he had wished he had taken.

Instead, he bluntly told me that he would have taken his physical health a lot more seriously. He felt that he taken his health for granted. In his words, he had treated his health like "trash," adopting a lot of bad habits that eroded his good health away. Above anything else in life, that was his greatest regret.

That was it. It was time to do something different for myself.

I've never accidentally eaten anything in my life. (And neither have you.)

I knew that—for me—fad diets weren't going to work. I tried a high-protein diet and I lost a lot of weight, but it became so monotonous that I dropped it. I am not a doctor or a nutritionist, but it seems that any diet that overly restricts the types of food eaten will inevitably become so boring that *anyone* will eventually drop it.

Staying in good physical shape requires attention to just a few basics. As far as I'm concerned, there are simple, fundamental laws that cannot be circumvented:

1. Avoid the poisons of smoking, drinking, and drugs.
2. Fruits, vegetables, salads, chicken, and fish are healthy. Simple carbohydrates and refined or processed foods aren't.
3. Enjoy desserts once in a while. They won't kill you. Just remember that, in most anything, moderation is the key.
4. Get adequate sleep to allow for your body's rejuvenation. I used to stay up late every night, but now I tend to go to bed early and get up early.
5. Eating right won't do it alone. Exercise is essential.

Everyone has his or her own way to stay motivated to exercise. Paramount, I think, is that you do what you enjoy.

For me, I've noticed that I'm easily motivated to go for a long walk or run when I'm near the ocean. For that very reason, I went to the extra effort of getting an office near the beach, so that I could keep my motivation up. Now, when I'm in the office, I eat lunch on the beach and go for a two-mile walk or run. Everyone has his or her own thing—these work for me.

I might never have the chance to be an "extreme situation" physical hero like Linda McSwain's father, but I do have the chance to be a "daily" physical hero to my family by keeping healthy. Being healthy affects the way you feel, act, and look as well as the quality of

Peak Physiology Training

Optimal performance occurs in the upper two quadrants of enthusiasm and calmness, while the lower areas of anger or depression have negative results.

Many students, athletes, and business people have become more aware of these kinds of relationships. Recognizing that the heart emits far more electrical energy than the brain, some now monitor heart rhythms and train in breathing and other techniques to shift their physiology and mindsets to the upper areas of coherence.

There is a clear connection between our physical bodies and our mindset. When we are in an area of peak performance, DHEA (Dehydroepiandrosterone, an anti-aging hormone) is released, while when we are depressed or angry, cortisol (a harmful stress hormone) is released.

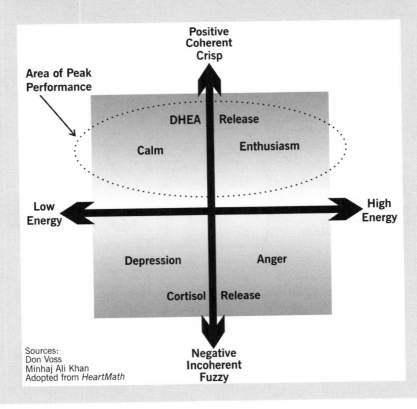

Elements of Good Health

Keeping in good health is a combination of eating right, exercise, and medical check-ups. Some people are adverse to seeing a doctor, which puts them at higher health risk.

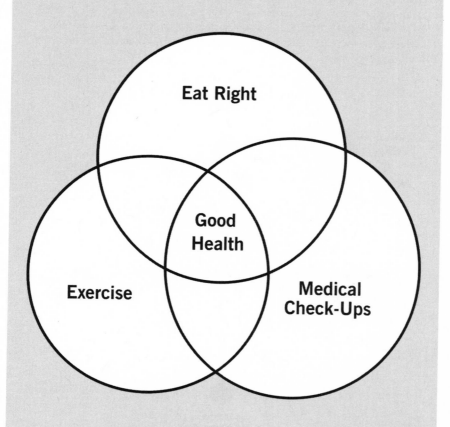

The Six "E's"

Just how "physically fit" is your business?

When it comes to evaluating the "health" of our products or services, business executive Curtis Reese created a great tool that he calls "The Six E's." One can effectively evaluate his or her product or service by simply completing the following statements:

1. Ethic - Our product provides value because . . .

2. Ego - Our product beats our competition because . . .

3. Enlightenment - We are educated about our product by . . .

4. Empathy - Our product satisfies our customers' needs because . . .

5. Empowerment - Our people are empowered to make our product or services even better by . . .

6. Enthusaism - We love our product because . . .

Courtesy of Curtis Reese

The elementary school clock, stopped at 1:05, stands as a memorial for those children who lost their lives in the "April Fools" tidal wave.

the role you fulfill as a mom, dad, student, leader or employee. This rings particularly true in a service-oriented workplace or daily situation where "the person is the product."

Just How "Financially Fit" Is Your Business Product?

When it comes to evaluating the "health" of our products or services, business executive Curtis Reese created a great tool that he calls "The Six Es." One can effectively evaluate his or her product or service by simply completing the following statements:

1. *Ethic*—Our product provides value because . . .

2. *Ego*—Our product beats our competition because . . .

3. *Enlightenment*—We are educated about our product by . . .

4. *Empathy*—Our product satisfies our customers' needs because . . .

5. *Empowerment*—Our people are empowered to make our product or services even better by . . .

6. *Enthusiasm*—We love our product because . . .

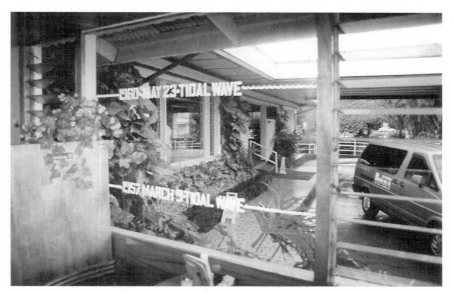

In Hilo, this local restaurant marked the water levels of two of the last century's tidal waves on the windows.

Being "Fit" Also Means Being *Competitive*

In both personal life and business, we must pay attention to our competition. Actually, we must create *barriers* to the competition.

Even the forces of nature can be competition. One awesome force of nature is the tidal wave, or tsunami. Tidal waves are large, rapidly moving waves triggered by a major disturbance such as earthquake, volcanic eruption, or underwater landslide. In deep waters, the tidal waves are only a few feet high. Even though they travel at speeds up to 600 mph, they cannot be detected by a ship at sea or even seen by aircraft overhead. Once they reach the shore, however, the sea can actually retreat for hundreds of feet, gather into itself and then . . . the waves come in. These are not foamy, friendly types of waves but, are rather a messy, slushy type. They advance and retreat over and over, towering as high as ninety to a hundred feet, equal to a ten-story office building.

Like tornadoes, the most disturbing aspect of tidal waves is that they are very difficult to predict. As an example, a few years ago, much of Honolulu was evacuated at a cost of millions of dollars because of a predicted tsunami. When the "monster" came ashore, however, it turned out to only be a few inches high.

We may chuckle at such an event, but it could have been serious. On April 1, 1946, a tidal wave that originated in the Aleutian Islands in Alaska, struck Hilo, Hawaii. Many people did not heed the tidal wave warnings on April 1, thinking it was an April Fool's joke. The waves reached an alarming fifty-five feet. Much of downtown Hilo was demolished and 170 people lost their lives. A schoolyard clock, frozen at 1:05 PM, still stands as a memorial to the place where many young lives were lost.

Sometimes, We Can Even "Beat" Mother Nature

While Hilo remains a popular location for tourists, the downtown district is always at risk of these large-scale natural disasters. Given the fact that tidal waves can hit Hilo again at any time, the physical infrastructure, then, must be unusually strong.

Consequently, some of the local hotels have ensured their "physical fitness" against this competitor by creating a unique "punch-through" design. When another tidal wave comes—and it is inevitable that there will be others—the hotels are designed so that the tidal wave can "punch-through" the lower levels of hotels that are now used for parking. Then, the hotel guests are not evacuated down to the ground, but rather go *up* through a "vertical evacuation" program where guests and staff can be rescued from the roofs by helicopters.

In order to survive, people just have to get used to the fact that they're going to have to deal with physical challenges. In Hilo, the hotel operators had every reason to give up and "throw in the towel." *Instead, they learned from the lesson, became more innovative on how to "beat the competition" and came up with a program that keeps their businesses open while protecting against the risk of tidal waves.*

Whether it's personal physical health or the health of our businesses' products or services, setbacks are inevitable. Dealing with them in an intelligent and assertive manner—that is, meeting the challenge head-on—is absolutely essential.

Physical Insights

- Few things matter more than being in good shape.
- Being in good shape *personally* means our personal heath and fitness. In *business*, our products and services are critical to the health of our careers.
- Threats to health are inevitable, so ensure against those risks.
- Many people will take heroic actions in extreme conditions, but the wise will take action each day.
- Knowledge about keeping fit and even the belief that a fitness concept works is of no consequence if this knowledge isn't put into action.
- There is no real shortcut to eating right and exercising.
- There is a direct correlation between our level of fitness and our mental outlook.
- Being "out of shape" is just slow suicide.
- Being rich and not taking care of oneself is just plain stupid.
- One should have a clear picture of how his or her product or service creates value, beats the competition, and satisfies the customer's needs.
- One should always be fully educated about his or her products and services and be empowered to make them better.
- When setbacks occur, it is critical to create innovations that work around the issue.
- A "failure body" is a sign of laziness.
- Markets pay superior rewards for superior goods.

Chapter Six

Environmental

Enjoy the View

Environments satisfy important aesthetic needs. Beauty, form, and balance are essential elements in both personal and business life. Billions of dollars are spent on landscaping, remodeling, and locating to or creating a nice environment—and rightly so. A clean and organized home and work area reduces stress and increases productivity. A beautiful view or a nice painting on the wall is inspiring and can be a catalyst to creativity.

Despite its importance, environmental issues have long been neglected by some, and much of my consulting work centers on environmental disasters. One assignment involved a small seaside community on the California coast called Avila Beach. This is a beautiful place, and many of the college students from San Luis Obispo come here on sunny days. The place is visually stunning. There are sandy beaches, a fishing pier, a golf course and some small shops and offices. In short, it is the perfect small California beach town.

Carelessness Often Snowballs into Enormous Disasters

On the south end of the town, a major oil company built some "tank farms" on a hill to store petroleum products. Literally running down the hill and through the main boulevard, a pipeline had been installed to pump the tank's contents to a dock and into tankers.

For years, the company pumped oil products through the pipeline, but only a portion made it to the tankers. Obviously, this meant that there was a leak in the pipeline, but nothing was done. This

Avila Beach before the town was shut down and excavated.

Avila Beach "after." Note that the tank farm on the hill has been removed and that much of the downtown is under excavation.

situation continued until hundreds of thousands of gallons had leaked under the town. *What would have been a relatively small issue to initially correct became California's largest contamination case.* The careless treatment of the town's environment has proven to be an extremely costly Left Line lesson.

The Aftereffects Of Stigma

Jeffrey Dahmer lived on 25th Street in Milwaukee, Wisconsin, where he was arrested for murder on July 22, 1991. He was convicted and sent to prison and later killed in a prisoner attack.

What was particularly disturbing about Dahmer is that he stored and ate his victim's remains within his apartment unit. Incredibly, one of his victims was found wandering and dazed outside, naked. The police came and, without any investigation, returned the young boy to his "friend" Dahmer. This careless police work not only resulted in the death of this boy, but in several more deaths to follow.

A private party owned the twenty-four-unit apartment where Dahmer lived. After the arrest, most of the renters in the other units quickly moved out, and within a year, the vacancy within the building

The Jeffrey Dahmer apartment site in Milwaukee, Wisconsin

rose to 83 percent. The building is located a few blocks from Marquette University. At the time of his arrest, a neighborhood revitalization program was underway by a non-profit organization called Campus Circle. Dahmer's apartment building was so disturbing that the agency actually paid a premium to acquire it so that the building could be demolished in an effort to enhance the neighborhood's environment.

Because of police carelessness, Dahmer's crimes continued and even got worse. Today, the stigma associated with the site is still so bad that nearby neighbors block the view of the vacant lot, and people cross the street so that they don't have to walk next to it.

Harsh Environments Can Force Even the Most Sensible Person to Succumb

The Heaven's Gate mansion is the site of the largest mass suicide in the history of the United States. The Rancho Santa Fe property sat on three acres, and the nine thousand square-foot home had nearly every amenity. The cult members rented the house; the lease specifically limited occupancy to just seven people.

The Heaven's Gate mansion had seven bedrooms and sat on 3.1 acres.

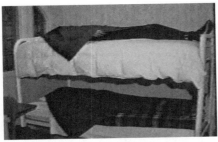

Police found thirty-nine bodies, with purple shrouds and Nike shoes in nearly every room throughout the house.

On March 26, 1997, police discovered the bodies of thirty-nine members of the Heaven's Gate cult. Bodies were found in nearly every room of the seven-bedroom house, and the first police to arrive at the scene were overcome by the stench of decay and body fluids.

The bodies were all located on beds or bunk beds, with identical purple shrouds over their heads and duffel bags by their sides. For reasons nobody knows, the cult members all had quarters in their pockets, and wore black trousers and black Nike shoes. The group left a "farewell video" in which they explained that they believed they were discarding their earthly "vehicles" to return to a spaceship that followed the Hale-Bopp comet. It was one of the strangest events in world history.

The general environment created by the cult was disturbing . . . even appalling. The cult's leader, Doe, clearly stepped out of bounds with the creation of a Right Line environment of harsh control.

The property owner contacted me just as the coroner's office was finishing the task of removing all the bodies. My first trip to the house was sickening; the smell was something that I will never forget, and I lost my appetite for days. After spending my first day there, I arrived back home and made a beeline for my backyard. I jumped in the pool with my suit on—I couldn't imagine the thought of taking that smell into my house.

When People Don't Think for Themselves

I visited the house on dozens of occasions, and each time I noticed something else more bizarre.

For starters, *everything* inside the house was labeled. Every light switch, electrical outlet, shelf, cupboard, jar, and container had a small label stating exactly what it turned on or what was contained inside.

This labeling extended right down to which light switch illuminated the kitchen sink. Initially, this preoccupation with labeling confounded me until one day when I was walking through the house with a colleague. She suggested that *Doe wanted to create an environment where all the thinking was already done.*

The cult leader, Doe, explaining the cult's decision.

Everything was done Doe's way. At the same time, no cult member was allowed to be alone. Monitoring devices were everywhere. There was a bizarre amount of wiring throughout the house and even down the chimney. Even when cult members spoke on the phone, someone was always there to listen in and monitor the conversation.

Every shelf, door, light switch, and bottle in the entire house was labeled. This shelf held coffee makers and enema kits.

*This extreme environment, along with the daily regiment, virtu-
ally eliminated the need for a person to think independently
about even the slightest detail.*

Ultimately, when the cult's leader announced that the males should get castrated and that they should all "shed their vehicles" to join a spacecraft, their ability for independent and objective thought had been completely eliminated. Consequently, thirty-eight other people died.

During one visit, I opened a kitchen cabinet to find a note taped to the inside with the eerie message, "We Did It!"

Mass Suicide Does Not a "Shrine" Make

While the press never knew it, the cult had sent a suicide letter to the home's owner. The tone of the letter suggested that they were actually doing the owner a favor by creating a *famous* event that would make the house an *invaluable* shrine. This was clearly yet another one of their delusions. In reality, they did the owner no favors at all. After the house was cleared of the bodies and their belongings, significant physical damage remained, which amounted to well over $200,000.

*Looking for some kind of break, my client tried to appeal his prop-
erty taxes, only to receive a letter in return from the San Diego
Assessor's Office that rejected his appeal on the grounds that a
mass suicide in his property did not qualify as a "disaster."*

Eventually, he was forced to give the property back to the bank. The bank, in turn, sold it at a deep discount to a nearby neighbor who promptly had the house bulldozed.

The point is this:

*Every environment has an impact on behavior. What surrounds us
can easily become part of us.*

If left in the wrong environment long enough, even the most sensible person can succumb to negative—even damaging—notions. Heaven's Gate was a bizarre environment that promoted bizarre

The Heaven's Gate mansion site today.

behavior. An important question here is, "Do *my* home and surroundings provide a positive environment?"

The same goes for our place of business, whether that is in our office, retail outlets, restaurants, or industrial facilities. The same question applies: "Does our workplace provide a positive environment?"

Harsh Environments Can Be Living Right under Your Nose—Or above It

While it's hard to imagine, those cult members had to have felt a measure of safety and tranquility or they would have found a way out. Some environments appear to be tranquil, yet they are actually quite harsh when you get past the facade.

Prior to its eruption, Mt. St. Helen's was a beautiful, towering sight. One local resident by the name of Harry Truman lived at the base of the mountain. Despite numerous warnings that his life was in danger, Truman only focused on the beautiful, tranquil environment and refused to leave. To him, the mountain was too awe-inspiring to really do damage, and he scoffed at the scientific data predicting a catastrophic event. Unfortunately, as Mr. Truman learned, *ignoring a dangerous environment does not make it go away.*

When the volcano blew, he was buried under hundreds of feet of debris.

Creating a *Comfortable* Environment Takes Conscientious Effort

When my wife and I started having children, we bought a house for our new family. It was big, bad, and ugly. It had been built in the 1970s and hadn't been updated since it had been built. There was dark chocolate brown and olive green everywhere, and it was depressing.

While in the throes of buying this house, I underestimated the impact this environment would have on us. As it turned out, we spent every hour and every spare dollar refurbishing it. Over several months, we got rid of all the old surroundings and replaced them with light and bright finishes.

Then another problem started. Having kids running around for the first time in our lives created piles of clutter everywhere, and it drove me nuts. A friend came up with the rule that each individual in the house had a room to call their own and that all their clutter got moved into these rooms. When someone's clutter was in his or her room, it eventually got cleaned up and, in the meantime, nobody else had to look at it. This idea worked, and the new environment at home made things a lot more comfortable.

Order Comes Intentionally

I work with a colleague who has offices in Honolulu. We met frequently in his conference room when I consulted on the Bikini Atoll nuclear testing case. During our first meeting, the conference room was somewhat messy. The meeting involved people from all over the world, and we were discussing a particularly important case involving hundreds of millions of dollars. I don't know if it was a fluke or not, but the meeting didn't go entirely well. One consultant got very irritated, and, at several points, the mood got angry.

When we met back in Honolulu for the next meeting, the conference room had been completely altered and looked very nice and organized. When I commented on this, my colleague told me that he'd had his office evaluated by a Feng Shui expert. Feng Shui is an ancient Asian belief system that suggests that certain environmental attributes have a positive impact on life, while other attributes are negative. Because of this expert, all the piles of documents were gone, everything was tidy and a small water fountain had been added to one of the corners of the meeting room.

I personally do not understand much about ancient Feng Shui practices, but I *did* immediately recognize that the atmosphere had improved noticeably. We had several more meetings in that conference room over the next two years, and all of them were friendly and productive. Was this just a coincidence? I don't know. I tend to believe, however, that my colleague's improved environment had some effect on our attitudes.

According to Feng Shui, a student will study better in a clean dormitory room, people will sleep better in a tidy bedroom, and a chef will prepare dishes more creatively in an organized kitchen. Furthermore, a mechanic will make repairs more efficiently with an organized toolbox, and employees will work more productively in a clean environment. In a sense, it can all be summed up in the old adage, "A place for everything and everything in its place."

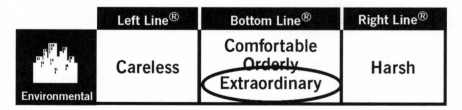

	Left Line®	Bottom Line®	Right Line®
Environmental	Careless	Comfortable ~~Orderly~~ **(Extraordinary)**	Harsh

When People Take Ownership of Their Environment, *Extraordinary* Things Happen

In recognizing the importance of the environment, the Dalai Lama advises, "Be gentle with the earth." This extends to urban areas as well.

One of the best examples of repairing a flawed environment and turning it into something extraordinary lies in the story of New York City.

My first trip to New York was in 1987 with a college buddy of mine. I had heard that New York was dangerous, but as a twenty-eight-year-old, six-foot-three, 225-pound guy from Los Angeles, I wasn't very worried.

I should have been.

On my very first night there, we saw gang violence, prostitution, drug dealers, a robbery, and even a murder. The murder was particularly disturbing as a man stabbed another man right in Times Square with police officers no more than twenty feet away. The bad guy got away. It didn't take me long to come to the conclusion that this place was nuts, and I left New York, never really wanting to go back.

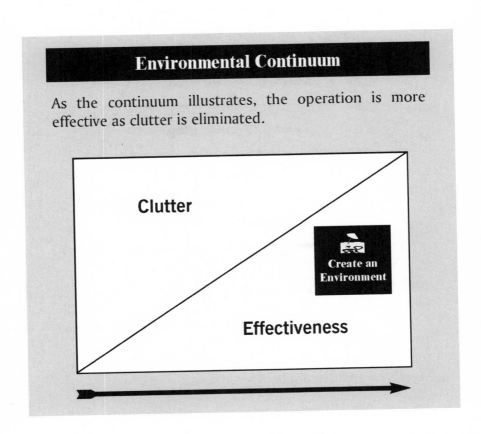

Environmental Continuum

As the continuum illustrates, the operation is more effective as clutter is eliminated.

Clutter

Create an Environment

Effectiveness

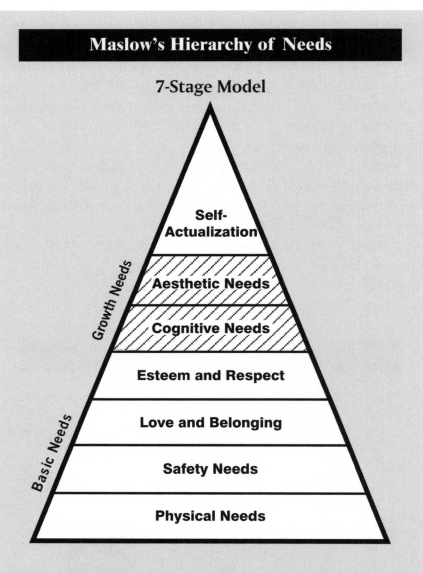

In the 1970s, Maslow's Hierarchy of Needs was modified by some to include two new categories, specifically Cognitive and Aesthetic Needs. Cognitive Needs include gaining knowledge and self-awareness. Aesthetic needs include gaining a better appreciation for the arts and creating a positive physical environment.

Years later, I heard that New York had been "revitalized," but I knew I'd have to see *this* with my own eyes. It was true—one of the most amazing urban reversals I've ever witnessed had taken place.

Mayor Rudolph Giuliani did the impossible: He cleaned up New York. He did it by cleaning up the outer environment first. Until then, the prevailing attitude had been to focus on the big, largely unseen problems, and let the "little" environmental ones go. Giuliani reversed this thinking by focusing on the small but visible things such as graffiti, panhandling, blowing horns, and windshield-cleaning extortionists. Walls were scrubbed clean, petty thieves and panhandlers were uprooted, and gutters and sidewalks were patrolled for trash.

In just a matter of months, the movement gained momentum and city residents began to kick in their own efforts. Somewhere in their conscious or subconscious minds, the residents of New York realized that they, as individual citizens, could help create and maintain a better environment. A change for the better no longer appeared to be so overwhelming. When their attitude changed, their environment changed as well.

A similar realization and processing was going on in the criminals' minds, too, except that *they* began to realize that they would get nailed for the little things, so they knew they would get nailed for the big things, too. Crime rates dropped like a rock.

Apparently it is the little things that matter!

Environmental Exercise

Use this worksheet to discuss what you enjoy about your current environments, as well as areas that you would like to improve.

Environmental Worksheet

	Like	Improve
Home		
Place of Business		

Environmental Insights

- What surrounds us can easily become part of us.
- The most sensible person may succumb to the craziest notions if left in the wrong environment long enough.
- Positive environmental influences—like water views, interior design, and Feng Shui decluttering—can make a notable positive influence on attitudes and behavior.
- Any environment that discourages or eliminates thinking is dangerous.
- Clutter is inevitably depressing and erodes efficiency.
- Do not be cavalier about known dangers that lurk in a peaceful-looking environment.
- Ignoring environmental problems will not make them go away.
- Little things can make a big difference in our environment.
- Students in clean dorms study more efficiently, chefs in organized kitchens cook more creatively, mechanics with organized tools work more productively, and employees in nice offices work more effectively.
- "A place for everything and everything in its place."

Chapter Seven

Financial
Apply the Banker's Secret

Bankers watch and manage their money like nobody else. They rightfully dismiss any "get rich quick" scheme. On the other hand, they know what builds genuine wealth.

The "banker's secret" is to understand the remarkable relationship between time and money and the power of compounding interest. To illustrate, if the Indians had taken the $24 in trinkets that they received in 1688 for the Island of Manhattan, and traded and invested to obtain a 7 percent annual return, today they would have nearly $6 trillion dollars, enough money to not only buy back all of Manhattan, but much of the real estate in the United States.

Bankers know the enormous power of interest. Interest earns profits around the clock, all day and all night. Bankers enjoy every moment, because they make money on the golf course, while they sleep and over the weekend. Lenders prey on the typical consumer who must have immediate gratification. The banker makes an attempt to extend credit at every reasonable opportunity.

To apply the Banker's Secret, we must flip the concept around for our benefit. First, we create something of value. Whether that is a product or service, we are compensated by the market for both quality and the effectiveness of its distribution. Then with the earnings, we must control spending and save a portion of the earnings, no matter how small. Rather than going into debt and paying interest, we earn it through savings and investments.

Those who know the "Banker's Secret" carefully budget their money, they reject impulse buying and dislike buying anything on credit and see paying interest as being toxic. If they do borrow at all, it is only for careful, conservative, and limited leveraging. They have less interest in looking rich, they want to build prosperity. They see the big picture. They know that their savings and investments are earning money every second of every day. This, in time, always creates wealth. And that's important because money does matter.

The scuba diving around the Bikini Atoll nuclear test sites is amazing, because the area is so undisturbed. Once, while coming to the end of my dive, I started my ascent with one thousand pounds of air, just as I was supposed to do.

Then I got distracted.

I caught sight of some pretty exciting things, including several poisonous lionfish and some sharks. With all the distractions, I used up the air in my tank faster than normal, and suddenly I was out of air. I was just about to drop my weights and bolt for the surface when my diving buddy handed me his "octopus," an alternative source of air from his tank. Everything was fine, and we calmly went up the side of a reef to the surface.

While I was okay, I will never forget that brief moment when I sucked and got no air. It was a lot like that feeling you get at the restaurant when your credit card is declined and you have no cash. It makes you realize that we take a lot of things for granted . . . until we run out.

I have had a friend since kindergarten who comes from a wealthy family. His father founded one of the country's largest restaurant chains. Once when my buddy was upset about something, I asked him how he could be unhappy when he had so much money. He replied, "Money never made anyone happy, but it's a great way to be miserable!"

There are those who, off-the-cuff, will say that "money does not matter." But let's face reality: they're just wrong. Money is a key ingredient to life. In the words of Woodrow Wilson, "No one can worship God or love his neighbor on an empty stomach." Money does matter.

Not being solvent and not being able to take care of one's financial responsibilities is over the Left Line.

Insolvency Usually Happens One Tiny Nibble at a Time

Fires, earthquakes, and hurricanes cause huge financial losses every year. One earthquake can split bridges, crumbles cities, and heave entire continental plates several feet. Hurricanes can tear apart homes like paper and leave miles of destruction in their path. I was once in the front yard of a house where a landslide had split it open as easily as you would crack an egg.

Fire departments are on constant alert to the damage that a blaze can cause. News reports will run for days covering the awesome damage caused by an earthquake. While these types of disasters result in spectacular damage, they do not even come close to the costs of one of the greatest disasters in America, even the world. The damage done by this disaster is incredible, ruining hundreds, if not thousands, of homes and businesses daily. It destroys fortunes and it's going on right now; but you likely won't find it on tonight's evening news. In fact, this tragic problem could be destroying your finances right now, and you may not know it . . .

It's termites.

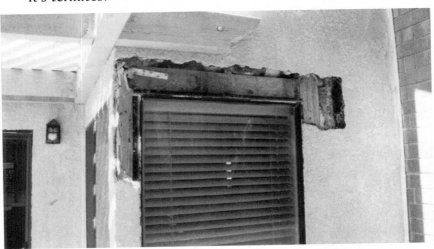

Termite damage is largely hidden and is often not known
until there is destructive testing.

Although small and often unnoticed, termites are relentless destroyers. All told, termites cause more than $1 billion in damage each year, year in and year out—far more than all earthquake and tornado damage *combined*.

There is an average of about thirteen or fourteen termite colonies for every acre of land, which puts about three or four full colonies near the average house in America. The insects have been around for 250 million years, and an individual bug can live up to fifteen years, longer than many animals. For much of her life, the queen will lay an average of one egg every fifteen seconds. With so many mouths to feed, the colonies are always looking for their favorite food—wood. It makes no difference whether or not it is wood from the forest or a house, termites love all forms. Their appetites are large and very destructive.

One can insure his home and business against storms and fire threats, but generally not against termites. Insurance companies are too smart—they know that the risk with termites is too great.

Comparable to the ongoing gnawing of termites is the disaster that gnaws away at your financial wealth—debt.

Debt is the "termite" that eats away at wealth and prosperity and can lead to financial ruin. There has never been a single instance in history of a bankruptcy occurring without debt . . . which accumulates slowly, quietly, and inconspicuously.

Which Economic Model Are You Living?

In dealing with financial disasters, I have developed seven economic models that illustrate the basic financial elements at play.

Types I, II, and III are okay.

The Type IV financial disaster occurs when revenues are rising, but expenses are increasing faster. This is the unspectacular, but slow and sure way to financial ruin. Yet it happens all the time. It's the type I see most frequently. The action of "spending less than is earned" cannot be successfully circumvented.

Type V occurs when expenses are higher than income, an obvious (and common) problem.

Type VI disasters occur when a calamity, such as a flood or fire, immediately wipes out a home or business. Insurance is obviously the best way to protect against this type of disaster.

Type VII financial disasters occur when income unexpectedly drops as a result of the loss of a contract, employment, or bad investment. Insurance is not the remedy here, and this is why all successful people and businesses must have a sensible mindset.

I once knew a man who had no college education, but had a solid, blue-collar job, a nice home, nice cars, and a pleasant life. Along came a "friend" who offered him the chance to invest and get rich quick. The scheme did not involve any of my friend's areas of interest or experience, but his objective was just to make a lot of money. He borrowed against his house and put all of his equity into the scheme. The rest of the story is a disaster. He lost everything, and, of course, the guy selling the scheme got everything.

Simply stated, moneymaking schemes make money, but only for those selling the scheme. I've never met a person who has become financially successful from gambling or from any get-rich-quick scheme. I have met some people who *do* get rich selling the schemes, but, with rare exceptions, the people who buy into them fail. The "get rich quick" mindset is inevitably a loser, while the "get rich slow and sure" mindset actually works.

As you look over these economic models, the key financial question is: "Are we earning more than we spend, and are our profits increasing?" History is riddled with examples of large and successful companies that squandered their assets and failed. Montgomery Wards, People's Express, and many of the dot-coms were all once promising companies. Today they're toast.

I once met a gentleman who made a fortune in high tech. By nearly any standard, he was set for life. He had experienced so much success that he believed anything he touched would automatically be successful. He started investing in everything that came along and . . . he lost it *all*.

Confucius said, "When prosperity comes, do not use all of it."

The Seven Financial Models

All people and organizations fall within one of seven financial models. Type I is the best, where income is increasing while expenses are decreasing. Type II has income increasing at a higher rate than expenses, and is also profitable. Type III has no real growth. Types IV to VII are all problematic.

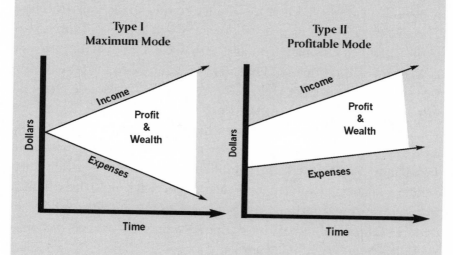

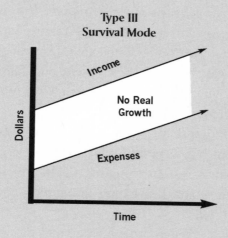

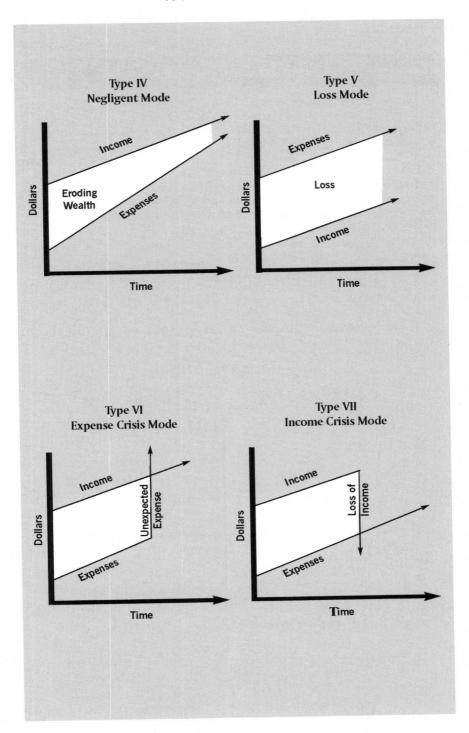

Profitability Tables

When evaluating business profitability, these tools are highly effective at determining where we are and where we want to go. Here, risk-reward, supply-demand, and cost-benefit concepts are organized in such a way as to reconcile commonalities between these concepts.

In all three matrixes, Q1 is the optimal target, where we enjoy high rewards and benefits, but with low risk and costs. This is where "cash cow" products and services are created. Proprietary Q1 situations can be achieved in a number of ways, such as being first to market, superior branding, licensing, technology, intellectual property (copyrights, trademarks, patents), business goodwill, and so forth.

In contrast, Q2 and Q3 are both in equilibrium, and so profits are somewhat "standardized" with profitability often being a function of good, effective management.

Q2 includes commodities and common businesses, franchises, the purchase of established businesses and partnerships. On the other hand, Q3 includes narrow "niche" situations with innovative or complex concepts.

Q4 are "turnaround" situations where we either reposition into Q1, Q2, or Q3, or drop the product or service altogether.

Risk-Reward Matrix

	High Reward	Low Reward
Low Risk	**QI** **+** **Proprietary**	**QII** **=** **Equilibrium**
High Risk	**QIII** **=** **Equilibrium**	**QIV** **-** **Distress**

Supply-Demand Matrix

	Low Supply	High Supply
High Demand	**QI** **+** Proprietary	**QII** **=** Equilibrium
Low Demand	**QIII** **=** Equilibrium	**QIV** **-** Distress

Cost-Benefit Matrix

	High Benefit	Low Benefit
Low Cost	**QI** **+** Proprietary	**QII** **=** Equilibrium
High Cost	**QIII** **=** Equilibrium	**QIV** **-** Distress

Ironically, *Greed* Actually Can Cause Major Financial Losses

A key to financial success is knowing not just when to be frugal, but also when to spend. Scrooge-like stinginess falls into Right Line behavior.

Some companies and firms delay a relatively small expenditure now to make the figures look good, fully realizing that there will be a major payback time later. In the Avila Beach case (chapter 6), a small, unattended leak eventually damaged the entire community. Because of the oil company's reluctance to spend a few dollars to fix a small problem, they were eventually forced to spend many millions of dollars, pay criminal fines, tear down much of the town, and excavate vast areas to clean up the mess. Often, doing anything is better than doing nothing at all. In this case, the oil company had plenty of money, but it went over the Right Line, played "Scrooge" and turned a small expenditure into a huge one. I see this same formula again and again.

A Small Problem + Inaction = Big Disaster

Many people and businesses mistakenly settle for the cheapest price or quote, but they end up paying more in the end to get things done correctly. As the old saying goes, "If you think an expert is expensive, try an amateur." One astronaut joked, as he boarded his spacecraft, that he was a little nervous about flying on a spacecraft that was built by the lowest bidder.

This sort of mindset existed with the Hollywood Boulevard sinkhole. The agency cut engineering costs, and the lower-grade engineers and contractors made major mistakes. Entire structures cracked and in some cases were condemned. Many of the famous stars on the Hollywood Walk of Fame cracked and had to be removed.

A Small Problem + Greed-Based Decision = Big Disaster

Where Money Goes Too Far

In my consulting practice, the situations we deal with often involve large portfolios, so my clients are frequently wealthy. One such client had inherited about $750 million. We were over at his

Major cracks in the famous Hollywood Walk of Fame resulted from engineering errors in the tunneling project below.

house, talking about business in his backyard, when the in-house nanny brought his six-year-old son out to the patio to say "good night." I expected the father to excuse himself and take a few minutes to go tuck his son in bed. Instead, from a distance of about thirty feet, the young boy waved, "Good night father" and my client yelled back, "Good night son," and the nanny took him right off to bed. It was only about 6:30 PM, so I asked him why his son went to be so early. He said that his son would usually read alone in his room for an hour or two until he went to sleep.

This event had a big impact on me. My little boys were about the same age as his, and our evening ritual stood in very stark contrast. We had an au pair to help with the kids during the day, but at bedtime, my wife and I would help our kids brush their teeth, get their pajamas on, sing them lullabies, read them a story, and have a prayer. From there, my kids would ask all kinds of questions about life and tell me more about their day.

There are certainly many things far more important than money.

$ Financial	Left Line®	Bottom Line®	Right Line®
	Insolvent	~~Generous~~ Budgeted Wealthy	Greedy

Generosity Is a Key Element in Any Good Financial Plan

Generosity and charity are essential elements of a strong financial balance sheet.

First, it's important that we be generous with ourselves. It is common in our American culture for businessmen and women to work like freaks in an effort to build wealth. This concept has grown so strong that the European notions of long, extended vacations sound bizarre. Being generous with ourselves means relaxing, taking vacations, going on walks, or taking trips to the spa.

It's also important that we be generous to others. The Bible urges people to be generous to those less fortunate—a lesson that *everyone* could benefit from. Good people and good organizations inevitably set aside some of their resources to help others. With many disasters that I see, I also see people who show up to help, whether they are people from churches, synagogues, charitable organizations, the Red Cross or just people who care.

I have noticed a trait among these people that always holds true: Those people who are helping others inevitably seem happy. I recall meeting a married couple in Kiev. When I asked why they were there, they told me they were spending a portion of their retirement years to help the children of Chernobyl. They were not with any organization, but they had come to live there and to help. They had calculated that for every hundred dollars they spent, they could save a child or dramatically increase a child's quality of life.

Budgets Create Solvency

One of my business partners, Mike Sanders, is my financial hero. He watches our firm's money like a hawk, is highly organized, and never wastes a dime. He takes the excess funds and puts them into short-term money market accounts so that we always maximize our profits and carefully invests our retirement funds where we will get the maximum returns. He is also completely honest. On many occasions, he has sent clients unused retainers from cases that are months or years old and that everyone has forgotten about. Mike has a natural aptitude for financial responsibility. Every organization needs a Mike Sanders to run productively.

Thomas Jefferson said, "Never spend your money before you have it." Living within a budget that reduces and eliminates debt will ultimately create wealth. It amazes me to see commercial after commercial promoting merchandise that anyone could live without, only to add a tag at the end about how financing is available. Many of these items are fairly small purchases, yet apparently there are enough people who just cannot wait to have them who will buy on credit. This approach is senseless. Benjamin Franklin said, "Beware of little expenses. A small leak will sink a great ship."

The key personal financial question to ask here is: "Do I spend less than I earn?"

While the ultimate goal of any business enterprise is to generate income, an issue that is actually more important than revenue is solvency.

When people visit Memphis, most think of visiting Graceland, the former home of Elvis Presley. The "King" died here on August 16, 1977. This small Disneyland attracts about 650,000 to 750,000 visitors a year. Graceland now earns more than Elvis did when he was alive.

Another important King is also associated with Memphis. On April 4, 1968, on a balcony of the Lorraine Motel in the downtown district, Dr. Martin Luther King, Jr. was assassinated. Soon after the tragedy, the motel fell into a state of disrepair. Eventually the building was abandoned and taken over by the homeless, drug dealers, and junkies. At one point, Dr. King's widow wanted the structure demolished.

The Lorraine Motel in Memphis, Tennessee

A wreath hangs on the balcony where
Dr. Margin Luther King, Jr. was assassinated.

Adam's Equity Theory

Relationships have a balance between inputs and outputs. For example, an employee puts in time, effort, and commitment to a job, while getting a salary, paid benefits, recognition, and vacation in return. The market "calibrates" what a fair exchange of the two should be. If the relationship goes out of balance, the situation must be reconciled or the relationship is at risk of breaking.

Market Calibration

Input   Output

Adapted from J S Adams Equity Theory

During his life, Dr. King made considerable progress in the area of human rights, yet more progress in this area was clearly needed. Until that point, there was no real central facility for the civil rights movement. Like any venture, advancing this cause would require finances.

Seeing an opportunity to both raise funds and educate others, the hotel was saved from demolition and renovated into the National Civil Rights Museum, which now attracts more than 160,000 visitors a year. Today, leaders and authorities from around the world give lectures and presentations there. The funds collected from the museum are used to educate thousands.

There are only three ways to make money:
1. Inherit money. With inheritances, though, comes the challenge of hanging on to the money.
2. Work for money.
3. Let your money work for you.

Given that the last two options are far more readily available to most of us, it is far better to let money work for you than to always be working for it.

With a conventional mortgage, a homeowner actually pays for his or her home more than three or four times. There is a common notion that high home mortgages are good because they are a tax write-off, but this is largely a myth. Even with the tax advantages of a mortgage, debt erodes wealth. From a financial perspective, while mortgages are often necessary, it is best that they be paid off as quickly as possible.

The first step in avoiding financial disaster is to live within a budget and to put part of every paycheck away in savings, so that money can work for you. No matter how small the paycheck, save some of it.

Benjamin Franklin said, "We may either diminish our wants or augment our means—either will do—the result is the same; and it is for each . . . to decide for himself. If you are idle or sick or poor, however hard it may be to diminish your wants, it will be harder to

Accumulating Wealth

The Power of Interest

Simply stated, the banker's secret is that they know the enormous power of interest. Interest earns profits around the clock, all day and all night. They enjoy every moment, because they make money on the golf course, while they sleep and over the weekend. They prey on the typical consumer who must have immediate gratification. The banker makes an attempt to extend credit at every reasonable opportunity.

The millionaire's secret is actually the same—just in reverse. Rather than paying interest, they earn it. While millionaires may not yet have earned their full millionaire status, they know where they are going. They reject impulse buying, dislike buying anything on credit, and see paying interest as a poison. They have less interest in looking rich, they want to be rich. No matter how small a paycheck, they always save a part of it. They see the big picture. They know that their savings and investments are earning money every second of every day. This, in time, always makes them wealthy.

$1,000 Savings Chart

This chart shows the incredible power of interest with only a $1,000 initial investment. Of course, if more money is added over time, the growth is even more staggering.

Years	Return: 4%	7%	10%	12%	14%	16%
1	1,040	1,070	1,100	1,120	1,140	1,160
5	1,217	1,403	1,611	1,762	1,925	2,100
10	1,480	1,967	2,594	3,106	3,707	4,411
15	1,801	2,759	4,177	5,474	7,138	9,266
20	2,191	3,870	6,727	9,646	13,743	19,461
25	2,666	5,427	10,835	17,000	26,462	40,874
30	3,243	7,612	17,449	29,960	50,950	85,850
35	3,946	10,677	28,102	52,800	98,100	180,314
40	4,801	14,974	45,259	93,051	188,884	378,721
45	5,841	21,002	72,890	163,988	363,679	795,444
50	7,107	29,457	117,391	289,002	700,233	1,670,704
55	8,646	41,315	189,059	509,321	1,348,239	3,509,049
60	10,520	57,946	304,482	897,597	2,595,919	7,370,201
65	12,799	81,273	490,371	1,581,872	4,998,220	15,479,941
70	15,572	113,989	789,747	2,787,800	9,623,645	32,513,165
75	18,945	159,876	1,271,895	4,913,056	18,529,506	68,288,755
80	23,050	224,234	2,048,400	8,658,483	35,676,982	143,429,716

Accumulating Wealth

Seven Points of Wealth

1. **Earnings:** Income is determined by the level of one's skill within the marketplace. Value is created by degrees, training, experience, and work.

2. **Savings & Investments:** A part of every paycheck is saved, no matter how small. The objective is to always earn interest, not pay interest.

3. **Budgeting:** The wealthy control their spending. The world is full of examples of those who have made fortunes and squandered it on reckless spending.

4. **Debt:** Credit is used on a strictly limited basis, if at all (i.e., student loans, home mortgages) but not for consumable items. The wealthy are disciplined.

5. **Insurance:** One must be insured against catastrophic events, such as death, disability, and major medical problems.

6. **Charitable Giving:** The genuinely wealthy always help others who are less fortunate.

7. **Trust Planning:** Smart parents have a plan to pass wealth on to their children.

Rule of 72

If you divide 72 by the rate of return (interest rate earned), it is about equal to the number of years to double your money. For example, if the interest rate is 10%, then $72 \div 10 = 7.2$ years.

Return	3%	7%	10%	12%
Years to Double	24	10	7	6

Rule of 72 — Starting with $100

Return	3%	7%	10%	12%
Starting	$100	$100	$100	$100
5 Years	$115	$140	$160	$175
10 Years	$135	$195	$260	$310
15 Years	$155	$275	$415	$545
20 Years	$180	$385	$670	$965
25 Years	$210	$540	$1080	$1700

Three Mile Island

augment your means. If you are active and prosperous or young or in good health, it may be easier to augment your means than to diminish your wants. But if you are wise, you will do both at the same time . . . and if you are *very* wise you will do both in such a way as to augment the general happiness of society."

Plan for Disaster

The Three Mile Island nuclear power plant near Harrisburg, Pennsylvania, had a nuclear meltdown as a result of a stuck valve. This was a risk calculated to occur once in 200 million reactor years. All things considered, that's a pretty reasonable risk and far less than the risk we all take every time we get into a car. Nevertheless, the best-laid plans can go wrong, and in the aftermath, the officials quickly acted, evacuating people and shutting the plant down just as a precaution. Despite being a big-name disaster, nobody was hurt and there was no long-term damage to the surrounding real estate.

The Three Mile Island incident shows that even the best and most meticulously prepared plans can go wrong, but that does not necessarily mean the end of the world. Being truly financially secure

The Global Matrix and Business Plans

The matrix is so comprehensive that it can easily accommodate any topic of a full business plan.

Business Plan Outline

PURPOSE	Philosophical	Mission Statement Type of Business (i.e, service, retail, manufacturing, sole proprietorship)
	Intellectual	Intellectual Property Logos & Branding Training & Development
PEOPLE	Sociological	Key Personnel Legal Structure (i.e., corporation, partnership) Roles & Responsibilities
	Influential	Key Contacts (clients, venders) Market & Competitive Analysis Marketing & Sales
PRODUCTIVITY	Physical	Product or Service Description Employee Individual Fitness
	Environmental	Facilities (offices, storefronts, industrial) Work Areas Home Office
	Financial	Earnings & Financial Statements Budget and Performance Break-Even Analysis Pricing
PROGRESS	Developmental	Goals Stage of Development
	Operational	Production Distribution Operational Flow Chart
	Consequential	Exit Strategy (Mechanism for Investors to Share Profits)

means having contingency plans for these events. Any individual or business that operates "too close to the edge," however, is asking for problems. A solid insurance program is necessary for both individuals and organizations.

For working individuals, disability insurance is often overlooked, but the odds of being disabled before retirement are much higher than dying before retirement. A tire blowout, a natural disaster or sudden illness can hit anyone and throw a life out of balance. I once consulted for the owner of a profitable business that had been hit by a major landslide. Prior to the disaster, he and his associates ran a very profitable business, but their property insurance did not cover damages caused by landslides. This was not the time for a lecture, though; this was a time for crisis management.

If You're Not Enjoying the Journey, Get Off the Train

We all know people who make a lot of money, but hate their jobs. I do not consider such individuals to be genuinely wealthy. My son Steven does not care much about money; he just likes his hobbies. On the other hand, my son Michael is very concerned with choosing a career that will make him a lot of money.

I tell him repeatedly to choose a career that he loves, and then the money will come automatically.

Confucius said, "Choose a job you love, and you will never have to work a day in your life."

Right out of college, I pursued business opportunities that were not that interesting to me, but that I thought would make me a pile of money. These did make money, but I was bored because I was not doing what I was really cut out for. I thought that becoming a lawyer would be more interesting, so I took the entrance exams, applied, and was admitted.

Classes were to start on the next day, and I was swimming in our pool with my family. I was just drifting around on a raft, wondering if I should really pursue being an attorney. The truth is, I was fascinated with damage economics, even though I had no experience in the field.

But I felt it would be interesting to pursue and pioneer the field. As I floated in the pool, I realized that becoming an attorney would be less risky, but pursuing damage economics would be far more interesting. In a decision that would change my life dramatically, I faxed my resignation to the law school the evening before classes started. And then I pursued what really fascinated me. I didn't set out to make more money, but I chose a field that I genuinely enjoyed.

For years, I did my work on a wide range of disasters without much notice, which was fine with me. But then somehow the media caught onto what I was doing. From that point on, my career has been profiled in the *Wall Street Journal* and *People* magazine; by the Associated Press; in dozens of other newspapers and magazines; and by ABC, CBS, NBC, and CNN. My career has even been the cover story for *Entertainment Tonight* twice.

I don't mention that to impress anyone. I mention it to impress *upon* everyone how important it is to find employment in a field of interest rather than to just make money. Media interviews are fun, but I enjoyed my career just as much before the media came along as I do now. I'm certain the media would have never paid any attention to me if I had chosen a career that I did not have any passion about. Choose a career you really enjoy, and financial success is inevitable.

Wealth Is Great, But It Has Its Limits

I once had some business dealings with a Hollywood producer. He had produced many major films and had been the president of a major Hollywood studio for years. Once we met at his office on the studio lot, and his walls were covered with photographs of himself with every imaginable movie star and political figure. His office was full of mementos that had been given to him by all kinds of famous people.

We then went to his house in Beverly Hills and sat in his private movie viewing room. Again, we were surrounded by mementos of his success. We had dinner served by his butler, and the two of us walked around his grounds and tennis court. He told me about his two famous and beautiful ex-wives. He took me over to a tree where a

Financial Pyramid

Many people make the error of driving straight for financial success, while not realizing that authentic financial success must be based on the foundation of strong philosophies, intellect, social responsibility, influence and contacts, strong physical and product attributes, a productive environment, and clear developmental and operational agendas.

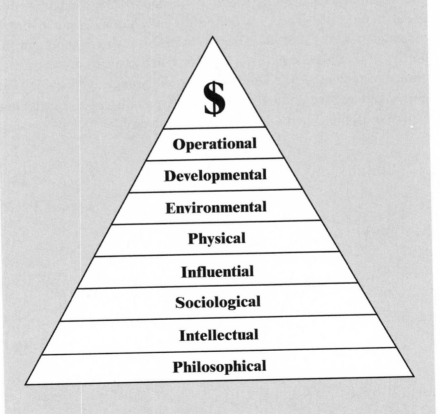

friend of his—a famous rock star—had gotten married. We walked over to the tennis court, and he showed me the umpire chair given to him by a famous movie star.

Soon the conversation took a personal turn, and he told me about how he had nothing when he was young and about major risks he had taken along the road to success. He started to cry when he told me about his divorce from one of his very famous and beautiful move-star wives, and how he had been at fault for putting movie projects ahead of her. He then told me something I will never forget. He said, "Randy, do you know what has motivated me to achieve all of this? When you're dead, you're dead, but my name appears at the front of dozens of famous movies, and in that way, I will always be alive!"

To me, this is a pretty sad view of immortality. My philosophy about money and success is quite different. Money is great—even essential—but it is not life. Like air, money is a vital component for life, but it should be kept in perspective. Once wealth is achieved, it is critical to remember the words of Andrew Carnegie, who said, "Surplus wealth is a sacred trust, which its possessor is bound to administer in his lifetime for the good of the community."

Financial Exercise

Using the format below, brainstorm with your fellow business associates on ideas to generate more revenues while cutting costs.

Discussion

Also, if you haven't already, formulate a personal budget that allows you to add to your savings regularly.

Financial Exercise

Revenue Generating	Cost Cutting

Financial Insights

- One must be solvent to have influence.
- In terms of necessity, money is right up there next to air.
- Even the noblest of causes requires cold hard cash.
- Solvency is more important than revenues.
- Compete on quality. "He that lives by the price shall die by the price."
- If you think an expert is expensive, try an amateur.
- Money is the closest thing to being able to store time.
- Choose a job you love, and you will never have to work a day in your life.
- Debt erodes wealth.
- "A small leak will sink a great ship."
- No matter how small a paycheck is, save some of it.
- When prosperity comes, do not use all of it.
- The best-laid plans can go wrong, so have a backup and a financial reserve.
- When faced with a financial crisis, doing anything is better than doing nothing.
- While money is important, it should be kept in perspective. It will buy a nice bed, but not a good night's sleep.
- People who are consumed by making money are dull.
- In business, net profit is the name of the game. In life, net saving and net worth are the name of the game. Everything else is smoke and mirrors.
- Surplus wealth is a sacred trust to be administered for the good of the community.

Part IV

Progress

Progress originates from the Latin *progressus*. The roots of this word are *pro* meaning "forward" and *gress* meaning "flow" or "movement," or "moving forward." The "action of walking forward" and the "advancement to higher stages" is taken by the *avant-garde* or "pioneers and innovators." "Progress" includes the categories of "Developmental," "Operational," and "Consequential."

Chapter Eight

Developmental

Pick a Target

Purpose, *people*, and *productivity* lead to *progress*. This is where passion is ignited. This phase is where we reflect upon where we are, see new opportunities and then take the challenge to break out of our comfort zones. From there, we go forward and discover new opportunities, raise the standards, and benefit others.

The best plans involve assessing those areas that are leaning most toward the Left Line or Right Line and making a conscientious effort to shift to the Bottom Line. In other words, we want to identify those areas where we are negligent and those areas where we have gone overboard, and then make adjustments and set goals.

When dealing with the topic of success, many people just charge right ahead to goal setting. Goal setting is good; in fact, it is a major topic of this chapter. However, note how it only now comes up now—after seven chapters. Before we go charging ahead with new goals, we must first take a sober look at our purpose, the people in our lives, as well as our level of productivity in relation to what we want. This prior assessment and information identifies our weak spots and lays the foundation for genuine development.

Turning Around *Regressive* Behavior

At the time of the Los Angeles Riots, I was living in Santa Monica, just west of Los Angeles. Initially, I was not too concerned from a personal standpoint, as I was miles from the epicenter of the violence. Curfews had been imposed, so my wife and I primarily stayed in our apartment. As the riots heated up, though, it looked like we might need to stay inside for a while. Since all the restaurants were closed, I went to the supermarket to stock up on some groceries.

When I got to the supermarket, I realized that I was not the only one with this idea. The market had not received any deliveries in days, and there were crowds of people buying anything in sight. I was surprised to see that the shelves were nearly empty, and the convenient and good foods were long gone. All that remained was stuff I'd never heard of. Looking over my options, I bought some canned baked yams and sugared beets. Then I got in the checkout line, which extended all the way to the back wall by the freezer section of the store.

When I got back to my apartment, the news showed that the riots were spreading rapidly. The area was looking like a war zone. Many roads were blocked, and I finally realized that we were utterly trapped with a burning police zone on one side and the ocean on the other. We had just a little food and no protection—and I was starting to get pretty concerned.

The Los Angeles Riots started on this infamous corner of Normandy and Florence with the mob beating of Reginald Denny.

When the riots finally stopped and the smoke and dust settled, the riots had spread to 21st Street, just eleven blocks from our apartment. Clearly, I had been negligent in preparing for an emergency. I was unprepared and was guilty of stepping over the Left Line. For years I had *intended* to get an emergency preparedness pack put together but, as we all know, "the road to hell is paved with good intentions."

In my consulting practice, I see that some people have not planned at all for a setback; or, when a problem hits, they have all kinds of mental blocks. They may lose their confidence, reflect on lousy experiences in the past or even revert to blaming their parents and upbringing.

Really, the past has only limited relevance. The relevant issue is where you are going.

Failure doesn't ask you to beat yourself up—it simply asks you to prepare more effectively.

Part of our development lies in realizing that some setbacks are inevitable. To achieve something great, we must be willing to fail along the way, at least temporarily.

If you place fleas in a jar, they will jump right out of it. If you put a lid on the jar, the fleas will jump and hit the lid, but after a while they will jump only high enough that they do not hit the lid at all. Their failure has conditioned them. Eventually, you can take the lid off, and while they are perfectly capable of jumping right out, their prior conditioning prevents them from doing so. This "conditioning to failure" impacts people too. In a crisis, some people feel so defeated by the situation that they sit and do nothing.

Setbacks aren't supposed to be necessarily negative. They're good for us. A setback causes change and prompts new action. Change wakes us up to senses and aspirations that may have gone dormant. Disasters can smash the entire mental and organizational framework that we're comfortable with and force us to face a different future. Vince Lombardi once said, "In great attempts, it is glorious even to fail." Failure only means that we are trying, and that we have moved that much closer to achieving our goals.

Nobody can become who or what they want to be by remaining where they are.

Some people are negligent in developing or setting goals, believing that they do not have the time. This excuse is weak. *If something will take five years to achieve, that time will go by, whether the task is completed or not.* If getting a college degree or a master's degree will take two or four years, that time will go by whether or not one goes back to school. As the old saying goes, "If you fail to plan, you plan to fail."

In some cases, when we look at the greatest successes out there, we may think of someone who is driven and passionate, pushing past every obstacle with wild-eyed pursuit and an almost irrational kind of thinking. This is not accurate. The true achiever has a keen sense of balance and knows when to back off from the extremes.

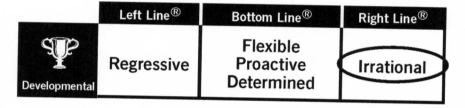

	Left Line®	Bottom Line®	Right Line®
Developmental 🏆	**Regressive**	**Flexible Proactive Determined**	**Irrational**

A Good Goal or an *Irrational* Goal?

While setting goals is worthwhile, there is a Right Line boundary to this process. As an example, the Menendez brothers weren't guilty of not having goals and objectives—they aggressively set a goal to achieve personal wealth and, at the same time, eliminate personal conflicts in their lives. On the surface, this sounded like a great goal. The Menendez brothers perceived that they had a problem, and they developed a careful plan to murder their wealthy parents. Had they kept their mouths shut, they might have even realized their goals and gotten away with murder. But their goals were irrational and obviously way out of bounds.

Often those who are trained in the area of corporate finance or sales will set numerical or quantitative goals. This is certainly fine with some types of pursuits, but this can also be a flawed mindset in some

Disaster Preparation

Effective goal-setting includes mitigating risk, so follow the *Strategy 360* framework:

1. **Philosophical**. *Get the Big Picture* and accept, "It can happen to me."
2. **Intellectual**. *Do Your Homework* and study *ready.gov* and *redcross.org*.
3. **Sociological**. *Think: Team Sport* and realize that emergency workers get overwhelmed, so ultimately we must be responsible.
4. **Influential**. *Get the Word Out* means communicating before, during and after a disaster.
5. **Physical**. *Keep in Shape* means there is enough water and food on hand.
6. **Environmental**. *Enjoy the View* means getting everyone to a predetermined safe place.
7. **Financial**. *Apply the Banker's Secret* includes having emergency cash.
8. **Developmental**. *Set a Target*, means having written plans.
9. **Operational**. *Make It Happen* and run the following errands:
   (A) **Camping Store**: Make 72-hour emergency kits. Purchase red backpacks or bags for each family member, plus each car. Get water filters, "camping foods," flashlights, radios, batteries and first aid kits. Also, put in cloths and medicines.
   (B) **Grocery Store**: Buy bottled water, non-perishable foods, and toilet paper. Plan for one-gallon-per-person-per-day.
   (C) **Bank**: Withdraw "emergency cash" for each kit.
   (D) **Computer Store**: Buy external disc drive, and back up key documents and photos.
   (E) **Copy Shop**: Photocopy key documents.
   (F) **Post Office**: Send external drive and copies to trusted person in another city.
   (G) **Gas Station**: Fill up, and keep tank at least half full.
   (H) **Storage**: Store kits near a door leading outside and in cars.
   (I) **Meeting**: Meet and discuss kits, plans, and emergency meeting place.
10. **Consequential**. *Leave a Legacy*, means passing along lessons to others.

The Menendez Brother's House

instances. Often, the better approach is to set one's head and heart right and let the numbers or scores take care of themselves.

Golda Meier was instrumental in founding the state of Israel and served as one of its first prime ministers. She said, "I can honestly say that I was never affected by the question of the success of an undertaking. If I felt it was the right thing to do, I was for it regardless of the possible outcome."

Rather than a business owner saying, "We need 20 percent more market share" or a charity or church saying, "We want a hundred new members or donors," a better approach would be to say, *"Let's do the right things for the right reasons, and the numbers will take care of themselves."* By doing this, the business is more likely to end up with 30 percent more market share and the charity might end up with five hundred more donors. Whatever the outcome, it will be better than if the action taken is only for the sake of numbers.

Some People Confuse Activity with Accomplishment

When it comes to both personal and organizational development, many Right Line people confuse activity with accomplish-

Where Are You?

Super achievers are inevitably pioneers in their field. The fact that they are the first to blaze a trail only serves to catch their interest and motivate them. Early users are risk takers who are high achievers as a consequence. The mainstream is average, while those who are idle or overly cautious end up as nonachievers.

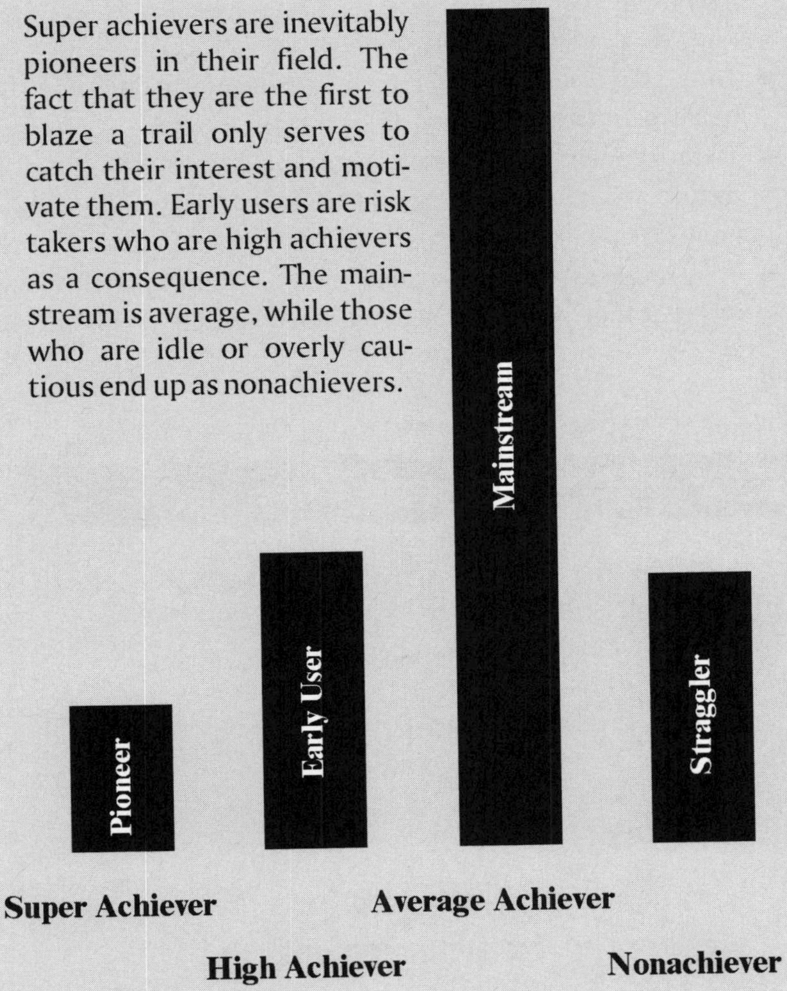

Adopted from the "Knowledge Acquisition Segments"
by Neil Balholm
Comteam Consulting

ment. Some are always busy running around, lulled into the illusion that they are getting a great deal done. One does not need to look very far to see such people; they are at work, in churches, synagogues, and community organizations. Would you, by chance, recognize someone with these characteristics?

- They tend to run around talking to everyone and they *love* having lots of "discussions."
- They crave meetings, lots of meetings.
- They talk frequently about all "we need to do," but their behavior sets no example.
- Their frequent meetings often go on without any clear agendas or objectives, and they rarely follow up on the commitments made in the past.
- They rarely take notes because they are so rushed with "activity" that they believe they don't have the time to spare.

The Activity Cycle

Activity for the sake of activity is of no value, if not detrimental. One must have a contentious plan in order to break the "activity cycle" and get real results.

No Plan

Activity **Activity**

No Achievement

Adopted from the "Activity Loop"
by Neil Balhoum
Comteam Consulting

- There is little follow-up to past discussions, just a constant discussion of future plans.

Bottom line, these people can waste extraordinary amounts of time and energy because of the irrational way they go about running *around* the actual achievement of anything.

Flexibility Allows for the Greatest Creative Achievements

Flexibility is an essential trait in the development and achievement of one's personal and business goals. For both strategic planning and crisis management, tools such as brainstorming are extremely beneficial when all those present are creative. There are some basic components to brainstorming successfully:

1. The problem must be defined and ideas for solutions need to be offered, but the session must be a genuine "free-for-all," where anything goes.
2. As ideas are gathered, there should be absolutely no evaluation, criticisms, or comments. The idea is to create an atmosphere where it is okay to say anything, be creative and think of the most out-of-bounds ideas, as these are often great catalysts to real solutions.
3. A designated scribe should be appointed to write everything down.
4. Once every idea has been presented, they can *then* be sorted and the pros and cons can be considered.
5. No idea should be tossed out until it is seriously considered. What might sound ridiculous on the front end can be a genuine stroke of genius once it's given its fair chance. Ultimately, the best solutions will rise to the top.

Another creative tool is "mind mapping," which is used to diagram ideas and concepts. This is helpful both in organizing one's thoughts and also in sharing ideas with others.

Mind-Mapping Tools

Mind-mapping tools can be an excellent way to both organize our thoughts and communicate them effectively to others. Many of these mind-mapping tools have been utilized throughout this book.

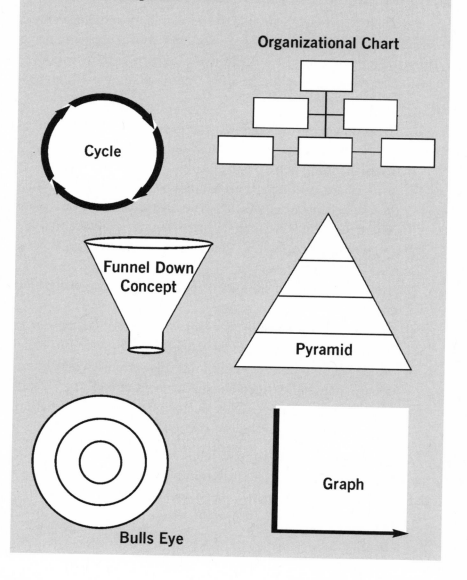

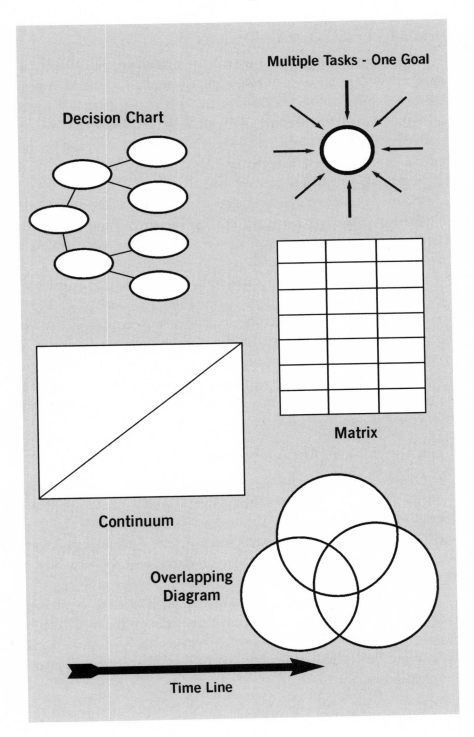

Flexibility Creates Greater Options

I had set a goal at an early age to earn an MBA degree. When I finished my undergraduate studies, I quickly applied to the MBA program of a middle-of-the-road university. I was not accepted. I was upset that I could not meet my goal within the time frame I had set, so I called the university and they told me that, because I had just graduated, I lacked business experience. I realized they were right, so I readjusted my goal and went to work.

About five years later, I applied to UCLA—a school that I had dreamed of attending since my earliest memory. I was accepted. Being flexible ultimately allowed me to not only achieve my goal, but to do so at a far better school.

One of the best slogans related to flexibility is to *choose your battles.* Enormous energy can be misdirected into the small stuff. A few years ago, I renovated an old office building. I am certain that I could have negotiated better deals from some of the contractors; however, at the same time I was negotiating business transactions that involved far more money. I knowingly accepted some not-so-great deals from some of the contractors so that I could move into the building and focus on my larger business agenda.

Proactive Thinkers Always Prosper

Everybody is in the business of problem solving. The computer industry exists to solve data management and communication problems; the auto industry exists to solve transportation needs; and the medical industry exists to solve medical problems. Homemakers solve the problems of running a household. Students must solve problems to complete their homework.

Whatever and wherever the case, problems should be viewed with an attitude of facing a challenge rather than avoiding it. A colleague of mine noted that the small problems never made him any money, but he welcomed big problems because they were profitable. Problem solvers prosper.

20 Questions

You can assess how you are doing by asking yourself these 20 questions, and then setting goals to move more into the Bottom Line area.

PURPOSE	**Philosophical**	1. Do I reflect on my core values, attitudes, and beliefs? 2. Does our mission statement and "business culture" reflect our ideals?
	Intellectual	3. Am I "teachable" and actively learning new things? 4. Are we actively training and learning as an organization?
PEOPLE	**Sociological**	5. Are my roles defined and do I meet my responsibilities? 6. Do we benefit clients and society, while creating barriers to our competition?
	Influential	7. Do I listen to others and is my voice heard? 8. Do we develop new business relationships and build existing ones?
PRODUCTIVITY	**Physical**	9. Do I take care of myself and keep in good shape? 10. Are our products and services in good shape?
	Environmental	11. Do my home and surroundings provide a supportive environment? 12. Do our offices and facilities provide a supportive work environment?
	Financial	13. Do I spend less than I earn? 14. Are profits increasing?
PROGRESS	**Developmental**	15. Am I progressing by setting goals, negotiating, and problem solving? 16. Do we have proactive strategic, marketing, and problem solving plans?
	Operational	17. Are my tasks prioritized and are my days organized? 18. Are our systems, operations, and meetings well planned and effective?
	Consequential	19. Do I learn from failures and celebrate successes? 20. Does our organization learn from failures and celebrate successes?

One of the most powerful developmental mindsets is what I call "The John Wooden Approach vs. The Phil Jackson Approach." I call these two philosophies the "score-driven" perspective (Jackson) vs. the "game-driven" perspective (Wooden).

John Wooden was not only an outstanding basketball player, but also the world's finest basketball coach; he lead his UCLA team to an unprecedented ten national championships.

Phil Jackson is another fine coach, who has led his teams to six NBA championships.

John Wooden sets out to "do one's personal best," while Jackson sets out to "win a championship."

Jackson's approach is obvious, effective, and a quick, easy sell; but Wooden's approach sets out a loftier goal and is ultimately more effective.

The Jackson Approach focuses on the score and "winning," while the Wooden Approach focuses on one's self development and the maximization of one's capabilities.

In our world, the masses are generally "score driven." These individuals and organizations focus singularly on the score, or "success." With this as their focus, the required attributes for building genuine value can be swept aside in the relentless and often elusive goal of capturing the all-important score.

On the other hand, the "game-driven" few are problem solvers who focus on maximizing their potential and playing the game to the best of their ability. It is not that they are unaware of the score, but their heads are truly into the game. They love to create value and they enjoy developing a great strategy. Ironically, success is the inevitable result of this approach, yet it is not really directly pursued. Abraham Lincoln said, "I can do the very best I know how—the very best I can; and I mean to keep on doing so until the end."

Walt Disney said, "Get a good idea and stay with it. Dog it, and work at it until it's done, and done right."

Decision Matrix Worksheet

The decision-making matrix can be very powerful in assessing priorities and coming to the right decision. The process takes just seven steps and has been used in some of the most complex decisions.

Decision Matrix

1. State the decision in writing

2. List the alternatives

3. List the key decision criteria

4. Weight each criteria in importance, making sure that the weights total 100.

5. Rate the alternatives in each category on a 1 - 10 basis.

6. Multiply each weight by the ratings.

7. Total each product to determine the high score. In this example, alternative B is best.

Issue: Where to move offices?	Weight	Alternatives: Rated 0 (Negative) to 10 (High)		
		A Ashby, IL	**B** Preston, TX	**C** Drake, NY
Cost	20	5 / 100	8 / 160	6 / 120
Labor Pool	25	6 / 125	9 / 225	8 / 200
Commute	5	3 / 15	5 / 25	2 / 10
Housing	10	10 / 100	6 / 60	5 / 50
Airport	5	9 / 45	4 / 20	5 / 25
Near Suppliers	10	9 / 90	7 / 70	10 / 100
Near Rail	15	2 / 30	7 / 105	7 / 105
Local Tax	10	4 / 40	8 / 80	5 / 50
Total	**100%**	545	745	660

General George S. Patton said, "If a man has done his best, what else is there?"

The effective mindset realizes that it is not a matter of what is accomplished, but what could have been accomplished had things been done correctly.

As individuals, we would be well advised to ask ourselves, "Am I progressing by setting goals, negotiating, and problem solving?"

In our business, the question would be, "Do we have proactive, strategic marketing and problem-solving plans?"

Nobody can hit a target that they do not have.

Goal Setting Is Essential for One's Development

When setting a real goal, one must first examine the basis for that goal by asking the following questions:

- Is this really "your" goal, or is it being done for someone else?
- Does the goal reconcile with your philosophical core values?
- Is the goal fair to all involved?
- Is the goal consistent with other goals?
- How will life or business benefit from this goal?

From there, the goal-setting process can truly begin. Here are some of the simple parameters I've followed:

1. *List all of your potential goals*, for every aspect of your life.
2. Review the list and *prioritize* the most important ones. Knowing that achievers focus intently on their top priorities, deliberately choosing the top goal, is of utmost importance.
3. *List all the obstacles* to achieving these goals, along with the individual task that will be required to get past those obstacles.
4. Most goals cannot be obtained alone, so *list all the people whose help you will need.* Ask, "what's in it for them?" Be prepared to present some incentives. This is an important one— and it's one I don't see in most goal-setting structures.

Goal Setting Worksheet

"A goal not written is only a wish." This goal-planning worksheet lays out all the essential elements of establishing and following through on goals.

Goal Setting Worksheet

1. State the goal in writing

2. Set a written due date

3. List every task that must be completed in achieving the goal

4. Prioritize each task

5. Set a due date for each task.

6. Check off each task as it is completed

Goal: Upgrade product   Date: May 15

		Task:	Due:
2	X	Sales force feedback	1-8
3	X	Customer feedback	1-15
6		Engineering feedback	2-7
5			
7		Compile all feedback	2-15
1	X	Form upgrade committee	1-4
11		New sales literature	3-5
10		Update product catalog	3-1
9		New package design	2-30
8		Get new product code	2-20
1		Prepare budget	1-4
4	X	Inform marketing dept.	1-20
12		Production	4-1
13		Distribution	5-1
14		Formal product launch	5-15

5. *Commit the goal to writing.* Writing down goals transforms a good intention into a real objective. *It defines the future and commits those involved to action.*

6. *Share your goal with others.* When the goal is written and shared with others, it is no longer another wishful resolution. Caution must be taken here: Generally, it's a good idea to share a goal with a good friend or spouse, but some types of "move up" goals should not be shared with anyone who may be intimidated by you reaching it, such as some coworkers or even superiors at work. They may not share your enthusiasm when your achievement could be perceived as leaving them in the dust!

7. *Break the goal up into small steps* and prioritize the steps.

8. *Crucially important is that you set a deadline for each step.*

9. *Start working the plan and be persistent.* Consistent and relentless effort has an awesome power. When the inevitable obstacles come, deal with them and move on.

Group Goals Have to Be Decided by . . . the Group

Goals cannot be successfully dictated to others. *In order for a goal to have any meaning, it must have authorship by those who are expected to meet it.* Too often, leaders will dictate goals without having the good sense to invite the input of those who are expected to achieve this goal. When this mistake is made, the rank-and-file workers, family members, or the organization's members will often shrug off this "goal." On the other hand, if they are invited to participate in setting the goal, the process has real meaning because those who are impacted have ownership.

Goal setting within my "groups" of work and family is important to me. I once met a family who had literally traveled first-class around the world for about three months. That sounded like a great event. Today, our family has the same goal. In the year 2011, our family is going to travel to all seven continents. We are planning all the sights we will see and are budgeting now for the around-the-world trip. We are planning the itinerary and we have a special account we use to save for it. The trip may seem like a long way off, but it will happen.

Growing up, I never considered myself as someone who was capable of writing a book. That seemed beyond my abilities. But then I learned a secret about achieving lofty goals. *I realized that if I did just a little bit every day, it would eventually add up to something.* I have written seven books, but this only adds up to writing less than one-quarter of a page a day. If we just hammer away at something a little at a time, our goals will ultimately be achieved.

Not Even an Atom Bomb's Destruction Can Stop a *Determined* Mindset.

Many believe that the plutonium-based bomb dropped on Hiroshima had been tested at the Trinity site in New Mexico, but this is not so. The Trinity site was home to a test of an implosion-uranium-based bomb, similar to the second bomb dropped in Nagasaki. But *the type of bomb dropped in Hiroshima had never been tested before*. Nonetheless, General Paul Tibbets commanded the first wartime nuclear strike in world history and dropped this first and untested atomic bomb on Hiroshima.

The nuclear bomb was detonated above the "A-Bomb Dome" and flattened everything for miles. Today the city is completely rebuilt, but the dome remains as a memorial.

Achievement Cycle

Many potential achievements begin with an intrigue of a situation that grows to excitement. After the "buy in," conflict and setbacks often set in. There is an inevitable critical juncture where the real level of commitment is determined and often one's character is tested. If truly committed, the individual will look at the situation more sensibly, implement a paced, day-to-day effort and over time obtain genuine achievement.

If one fails at the critical juncture, then disillusionment or even hostility can set in.

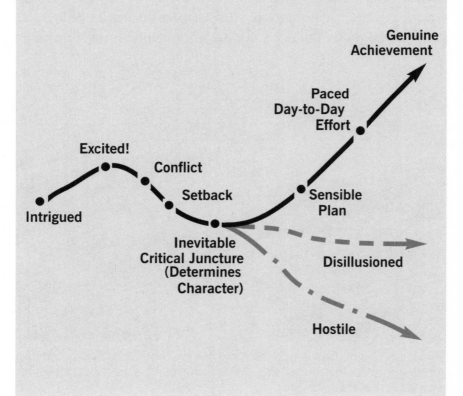

General Tibbets told me that, when the bomb went off, the blast was so bright, he put his hands over his eyes and saw the bones of his hands.

Hiroshima had been chosen as a target because it was an industrial city that had an important role in the war effort. At that time, the city had not been bombed, so it would be easier for the Japanese to see the devastating damage.

I once gave a lecture to an alumni association, and the mayor of a large city sat at the head table. I commented that the mayor must be facing major challenges, but that it was hard to imagine a more devastating problem for a city than having an atom bomb dropped on it. Yet, this is exactly what happened to Hiroshima.

Despite the bomb's stunning effect, today's Hiroshima stands in stark contrast to the sites of many major disasters I've researched. As an example, I was invited to lecture at a conference in South America and, while there, I toured a large cathedral damaged by the great Chilean earthquake in 1960, the largest earthquake in recorded history. The repair efforts are still going on today, more than forty years later.

Not so for Hiroshima. It is a completely developed, clean, and efficient city. The only physical reminder of that fateful day is the Peace Memorial complex, which centers around the famous A-Bomb dome, a former industrial facility at the hyper-center of the explosion. A skeleton of the building remains today, which is the focal point of a large complex. An enclosed bridge links two identical buildings that serve as a modern convention center and a museum. In fact, when I was walking to the museum, I accidentally walked to the wrong end and into a shoe convention.

Even this complex reminds me of the mindset of moving forward. On one end, visitors come to view exhibits related to the bomb, while just yards away, other people come to attend various business conventions. I think this is a phenomenal symbol of looking to the lessons of the past, while also looking to the business of going forward.

The people of Hiroshima were dealt an unprecedented blow. Yet, they did what they could to solve the problems and move on. *One of the most fascinating aspects of Hiroshima was the resolve of the people to move forward in the rebuilding of their city—an effort that commenced only two days after the bomb had been dropped.* Hiroshima illustrates that, even under the most extreme hardships, it is those who are able to overcome the problems who create value and prosperity.

> *The Japanese understood that it's not where you start . . . it's where you go.*

They avoided the temptation to become "the victim." The mindset and culture of the people aggressively solved problems instead of dwelling on them. In fact, one Hiroshima teenager told me that, while he was aware of World War II and "the bomb," he was unaware that it had been dropped on Hiroshima. This is evidence of the success they've had in putting the past behind them in order to create a better future.

Persistence and dogged determination is a common mindset among those who overcome obstacles and achieve success.

The key attitude of a winner is captured in the statement of Vince Lombardi, who said, "It's not whether you get knocked down . . . it's whether you get up." The Japanese people who survived Hiroshima understood that. As long as we get back up after a failure, we are, by definition, a "winner."

Lombardi added, "The difference between a successful person and others is not a lack of strength, not a lack of knowledge, but rather a lack of will." Lombardi was just like the rest of us—he lost some games. But he always got back up and went at it again.

Another Key Developmental Skill Is Negotiation

We never stop negotiating.

We negotiate with our spouse over where to live, the household budget, what cars to buy, where to go for vacation, and sometimes even where to spend the holidays.

In business, we negotiate our salaries and bonuses, as well as deals with clients, vendors, and others.

One of the worst setbacks any of us can suffer is the act of being out-negotiated and leaving money on the table. I was a consultant to a lawsuit where the defense was willing to pay $5 million dollars to settle the case, but the plaintiff's attorney was a lousy negotiator and settled, instead, for just a few hundred thousand dollars. As a consultant for the defense, I was elated.

Many of the disasters I'm retained to study involve situations where millions or even billions of dollars are at stake. Many people think that there are some complex and secret negotiation strategies, and that they only get more complex and secret the higher the money value is surrounding the negotiation. This is completely untrue. Negotiation concepts are actually very basic.

If we keep nothing else in our heads about negotiation, just remember these two key thoughts: "Time is money," and "Choose your battles."

While it may be worthwhile to negotiate a lower fee from a vendor ("time is money"), it may be a bad idea to negotiate for a cheaper couch than the one your spouse likes ("choose your battles."). Trust me—I tried that once.

Rules of Play in Negotiation Are Simple and Never Changing

If it is something that is really worth negotiating, take some time and do your homework. Here are some quick pointers on negotiation:

- Check out your opponent and all the options.
- Listen carefully.
- Keep your mouth shut. Saying too much too fast blows many negotiations.
- Let the other side throw out the first number and no matter what it is, shake your head and give a big sigh. Deflate your opponent's expectations right away.
- Remember this: You have more power than you think. When buying something, generally you have all the power; the sales-

man's power is just an illusion. (Or, at least that's the best mindset to have as a buyer.)

- Keep track of your incremental progress toward reaching a deal. If your opponent drops a dollar, then you raise only twenty cents. While appearing accommodating, this keeps the incremental process balanced in your favor.
- Above all, remember that the big decision is usually made in the final moments. Play any deadlines or other issues of timing to your advantage.
- As Margaret Thatcher once said, "You may have to fight a battle more than once to win it." If you want it, don't stop negotiating.

One-Liners That Put You in the Negotiation Driver's Seat

There are some great "one-liners" for negotiation:

- "I never argue with my competitor's low prices; we compete on quality."
- "If you think an expert is expensive, try an amateur."
- When a rule or policy is laid out that you are expected to obey, just say, "That doesn't apply to me in this case."
- "I love your product or idea, but you've got to do better than that."
- "I've gotta go."

A friend of mine once purchased a new car and did no negotiating. I purchased the exact same car and saved more than $14,000 in just two hours of time. My friend just went in and bought the car. I went in and spoke to the salesman. Here's how the negotiation proceeded from there:

His action: Of course, the salesman was anxious for me to buy the car right then. In fact he used the old sale's pitch, "What can I do to get you to buy this car right now?"

My action: I just smiled and took his best price to another dealer and the Internet, where I quickly got better prices.

His action: When I took this information back to the salesman, he was forced to offer me a much better deal, "if I bought right now."

My action: I didn't understand the urgency of purchasing the car "right now," so I told him I would think about it. I called him on the phone a few times.

This did five things:

1. He knew I was genuinely interested rather than just looking.
2. It forced him to "invest" some time in the sale, which made him want to work hard to get a return on his time "investment."
3. It just wore him out. Once I got him ground down to a point where the price could not get any lower, I agreed on the price, but then started adding features to the car until it was loaded.
4. I also waited until the last day of the month, so that I could capitalize on the timing of his month-end numbers. Even then, I waited until late at night to really put the pressure on him.
5. I believe that *as long as the salesman is smiling, I need to keep negotiating*. At a point where this salesman's smile disappeared altogether, I realized that I had pushed my luck as far as it would go and bought the car.

All told, it was definitely worth the $7,000-per-hour savings.

Developmental Insights

- Problem solvers progress.
- We are all in the "business" of problem solving.
- It's not where you are; it's where you are going.
- All of your life will be spent in the future.
- A goal not written is only a wish.
- Small problems never make much money.
- Whenever one gets up after getting knocked down, they are, by definition, a winner.
- Persistence is the common trait among those who overcome obstacles.
- Goals are important, but they must align with our philosophical core values.
- Activity does not equal accomplishment.
- One's conditioning may place artificial barriers on their aspirations. To develop, we must conscientiously destroy these false mental boundaries.
- "Doing one's personal best" is a superior developmental philosophy to "winning."
- There is no central theme to success, only a balance of a variety of attributes.
- Failure must be viewed as only a temporary event and not a conclusion.
- Do the right things for the right reasons, and the numbers will take care of themselves.
- New Year's resolutions can be made at any time of the year.
- The question "How well did we do?" is better asked, "How well *could* we have done this, if we had done it right?"
- Successful goals can never be dictated, but rather are a team decision by those who are expected to achieve them.
- When you negotiate, you often have more power than you think.
- As long as the salesman is smiling . . . keep negotiating.
- "Failure" should always be regarded as a temporary event.

- Setbacks and criticism provide the fuel for the use of problem-solving skills to generate growth.
- Problem solvers are proficient with the tools of brainstorming, goal setting, negotiation, and decision making.
- The non-achiever believes that his failures have happened for the first time in history.
- Like lifting weights, a task will get easier and easier over time.
- Everyone has a dream. Conrad Hilton said, "You must have a dream if your dream is to come true."
- Nobody would build a doghouse without a plan, yet there are those who will turn around and start a business without any business plan.
- There is a "try" in every triumph.
- Every business started as the idea of one person
- Don't focus on stopping bad habits, focus on implementing good habits. Good habits force out the bad ones.

Chapter Nine

Operational

Make It Happen

For centuries, many emphasized the avoidance of the "Seven Deadly Sins," specifically, pride, envy, gluttony, lust, anger, greed, and sloth." Around 1730, while in his late twenties, Benjamin Franklin took a positive view and—rather than worrying about what not to do—he listed thirteen virtues that he wanted to proactively pursue in his everyday activities.

Franklin placed each of the virtues on a separate page of a small book and focused on that virtue for a full week. He evaluated his performance daily. Franklin emphasized these virtues in his Poor Richard's Almanac, (which included the famous advise to his son William, "all work and no play make John a dull boy.")

Benjamin Franklin's 13 Virtues

1 **Temperance**: Eat not to dullness; drink not to elevation.

2 **Silence**: Speak not but what may benefit others or yourself; avoid trifling conversation.

3 **Order**: Let all your things have their places; let each part of your business have its time.

4 **Resolution**: Resolve to perform what you ought; perform without fail what you resolve.

5 **Frugality**: Make no expense but to do good to others or yourself; i.e., waste nothing.

6 **Industry**: Lose no time; be always employed in something useful; cut off all unnecessary actions.

7 **Sincerity**: Use no hurtful deceit; think innocently and justly, and, if you speak, speak accordingly.

8   **Justice**: Wrong none by doing injuries, or omitting the benefits that are your duty.

9   **Moderation**: Avoid extremes; forbear resenting injuries so much as you think they deserve.

10   **Cleanliness**: Tolerate no uncleanliness in body, cloths, or habitation.

11   **Tranquility**: Be not disturbed at trifles, or at accidents common or unavoidable.

12   **Chastity**: Rarely use venery but for health or offspring, never to dullness, weakness, or the injury of your own or another's peace or reputation.

13   **Humility**: Imitate Jesus and Socrates.

Success is the result of putting our priorities into action. It's one thing to set goals and another to get the job done. Once we define our purpose, assess our relationships and level of prosperity, and set our objectives, it all comes down to the day-to-day activity and the effective use of our time. In day-to-day life, the achiever will have a keen sense of when to be passive, active, or aggressive. Having the most ingenious plan will mean nothing if priorities are not actually integrated into our lives. Putting time into the important tasks is where the "rubber meets the road."

Sometimes surprises come along, and those who achieve will know when to put other matters aside and put their problem-solving skills into action. Indeed, putting off the inevitable is at the heart of many problems I see daily.

The Laguna Niguel landslides in Southern California on March 19 and 20, 1998, started off looking like a pretty minor case. Over the course of two days, however, seven houses dropped 125 feet in a spectacular—and televised—landslide.

What the media did not report was that the landslide actually had begun several months prior in one home, starting with a quarter-inch crack between the ceiling and a laundry room cabinet. In California, there is a ten-year statute of limitations for construction defects. Based on this apparently small amount of damage, attorneys for the homeowners filed suit just one day before the statute of limitations expired.

Negligent Operation Creates Even a Bigger Problem

I was hired in this case months before the dramatic landslides. I have seen several landslides, but these were in a league of their own. An old trick with structures suspected of sitting atop soil problems is to put a marble on the floor. If it rolls, it's a potential sign of what geotechnical engineers call "differential settlement," or what the rest of us of call a "tilted floor." In this case, not only did the marble roll, but windows cracked, mirrors shattered, walls pulled apart and doors broke off their hinges, all right before our eyes.

Little did we know that the six-inch crack was about to widen to 125 feet—literally—within the next twenty-four hours. When I saw that landslide, I was very relieved that it didn't occur the day before—when I was in the house!

Before that slide, all of the geotechnical experts agreed that the hillside would eventually fall in a catastrophic drop. Several measures could have been taken to limit the damage. As John F. Kennedy said, "The time to repair the roof is when the sun is shining." Despite the oncoming predicted disaster, the developers and their attorneys did nothing—a classic Left Line sign of negligence.

The homes in Laguna Niguel before the landslide

After the Laguna Niguel landslide

A much smarter reaction would have been to accept the inevitability of the situation, purchase the homes from the owners, dismantle them, and salvage the scrap. Then, when the landslide occurred, it would have affected nothing more than some vacant lots, which is hardly a newsworthy event. Of course, none of this occurred, which was the developers' first mistake.

The developers' mistakes were further compounded with a "no comment" response. Right or wrong, in the eyes of the public, "no comment" often means "I'm guilty." Finger pointing and hiding in a hole is generally the worst way to handle a crisis.

A much better response? Just deal with it.

How to Know When It's Time to Be Proactive

Theodore Roosevelt said, "Take action, seize the moment. Man was never intended to be an oyster." Inaction from both the developers and their attorneys provided the fuel for hundreds of hours of broadcast time, during which the nation was repeatedly reminded of their mistakes.

Although this situation involved a dramatic landslide, its lessons are applicable to everyday problems. When a copier breaks down, the time to fix it is immediately, not when an important document needs to be copied. When a car tire is worn out, the time to replace it is immediately, not when it goes flat and you're stranded by the side of the road. When a child demonstrates aggressive behavior, the behavior must be dealt with immediately, not when he goes to prison. A sloppy employee should be dealt with quickly, before the business suffers.

In situations where trouble is inevitable, any actions short of being proactive will surely result in the damages being amplified. Taking action in the face of a crisis is certainly important, but there are those situations where the simplistic adage, "be proactive," can be unrealistic. No one can be proactive on all fronts at all times. Rather, I've noted that effective people make decisions on when it is best to be *proactive* or when being *reactive* is best. In other words, sometimes it's best to simply react to smaller problems, while actively taking charge of the more important ones. Planning those high-priority items into one's daily operation is essential. In fact, success *is* putting priorities into action.

Compulsive Behavior Can Be Worse Than Negligence

In a strange way, the importance of prioritizing one's daily operations was clearly illustrated with the problems at Tiananmen Square, where the Chinese government shot and killed dozens during a student protest.

I visited Tiananmen Square on the ten-year anniversary of the massacre. I didn't know what to expect, and I was nervous about my first trip to a Communist county. *My concerns were not alleviated when I stepped off the plane and saw machine-gun toting soldiers at the foot of the stairs.* The airport was old, gray, cold, and drab. When I exchanged money, the people working in the room looked absolutely hopeless. The taxi was a battered old car with ripped seats. This was not looking good.

I wanted to dig in, do some research and ask a lot of tough questions, but I also didn't want to end up in a Chinese water-torture cell for doing it.

Fortunately, the view improved when I saw billboards for TGI Friday's and McDonald's on the highway. By time I checked into my Hilton Hotel, I was feeling a little more comfortable.

China: A Home for Millions of "Common People"

China is a fascinating place. I watched from my hotel room for hours as literally hundreds of *thousands* of people, all dressed nearly identically in dark gray clothes, rode bikes or hustled on their feet on the boulevard below. These people were the machines that kept the country running, but they did not seem particularly happy about it. I never saw a unique piece of colorful clothing, and I never saw a smile.

I spoke to many students involved in the incident. Contrary to the Western media, they considered the protests to be more a protest against corruption in the government, not necessarily about democracy. In fact, many of the students I spoke with had only a limited knowledge or interest in the subject of democracy.

I learned that there are many other misconceptions about the Tiananmen Square massacre:

The number of people killed is unknown, but most credible sources agree that it was far less than the 4,000 reported by some of the media. It was probably in the dozens or hundreds.

- The massacre did not occur on the square at all, and there is not even one confirmed death that occurred there.
- The bloodshed was actually on the streets that led to the square.
- Most surprising—as I dug deeper, it became apparent that most of the people killed were not students at all, but were "common people" who where trying to keep the army from getting to the students. Even in China, students are allowed a certain amount of leeway in thought and behavior that is not afforded to the common workers. From the Communist gov-

ernment's point of view, they could tolerate some discussion and even protests from the students, but they would *not* tolerate any rebellion from the rank-and-file "common people." If this were allowed, the government felt that it would too easily lose control of the country—if some people got away with it, the rebellion could spread uncontrollably.

In a tragic and compulsive way, China's Communist government confirmed an important fact: *The fundamental operations of an organization cannot be disrupted without causing serious harm.* In an obsessive Right Line way, the Chinese government recognized this. Once their daily operations were at risk, they stepped in to stop it.

An *Easygoing* Attitude Can Actually Be Good Bottom Line Thinking

Among other things, disasters certainly demonstrate that the unexpected can happen anytime, so maintaining a flexible mindset is essential. We would all drop anything in the event of a flood or fire, but how about helping out someone else who is in trouble?

I once heard about a man who was on the way to a job interview. The traffic was backed up a little, and he eventually came upon a woman who was stranded in the middle of the road with car trouble. Other motorists were honking and annoyed at this woman. The man decided to help. He pulled over and pushed her car over to the side of the road, then offered his cell phone to call for help. The woman first called a tow truck, then dialed his own cell phone number.

It turned out this woman was the CEO of the firm where the man was interviewing, and she was the person with whom he was going to meet. No surprise, this man's flexibility resulted in him getting the job.

It's been said that our true character is revealed by how we treat others who can neither help nor hurt us.

Easygoing Flexibility Applies to Personal Life, Too

When my wife and I bought our current house, we were anxious to remodel and set a rigid deadline for getting it done. Even with our self-imposed deadline, we were somewhat sporadic in our remodeling until the job became so frustrating that it was clear we did not have our remodeling priorities in the right order. As an example, we spent a lot of time getting quotes to redo the floors because they bothered us the most. As time went on, it became obvious that it wouldn't be smart to put nice floors in first, only to have them destroyed by subsequent construction. We then overhauled our priorities and extended our deadline significantly.

The "Hang Loose" Formula

Flexibility is essential. Some problems are simply too much to do anything about, so just "waiting it out" might be the preferred way to go. This smart strategy was seen at the Manoa Landslides in Hawaii, a premier area where many of the homes have an outstanding view of downtown Honolulu and the ocean.

There are two basic types of landslides—the fast, spectacular type and a very slow type. Manoa's landslides were the slow type. The slow-moving slippage had caused the ground to heave or sink several feet over a period of several months or even years.

The Manoa Landslide completely destroyed some houses
and left others like this one partially sunken.

The Paty-Alani and the Hulu-Woolsey landslides damaged and destroyed approximately 150 of 600 homes. Unfortunately, the remaining 450 homes, while not damaged at all, suffered from the reputation of the area. Over a nine-year period, only seven homes sold in an area where normally dozens of homes would have sold each year.

Many residents applied one of the best philosophies around: When a problem hits, don't panic. Just kick back, wait it out and avoid taking the loss. Indeed, the city made repairs and things did get better over time.

Meanwhile the residents found better things to do with their time.

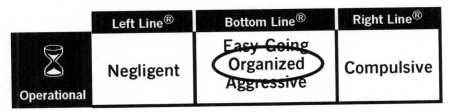

We All Have the Same Number of Minutes to Keep *Organized*

Time management dictates that we personally ask, "Are my tasks prioritized? Are my days organized?" Within our organizations, we need to ask, "Are our systems, operations, and meetings well-planned and effective?" Prioritization might seem an overwhelming task, but as Abraham Lincoln said, "The best thing about the future is that it comes only one day at a time."

As the business executive Chris Ramsey said, *"Time is the great equalizer."*

We all have the same number of minutes and hours in a day, no matter our nationality, wealth, age, or education.

The achiever looks at time as a highly valuable and non-replaceable commodity and is careful what he or she does with it.

Theodore Roosevelt said, "Far away the best prize that life offers is the chance to work hard at work worth doing." I believe that Roosevelt was not only referring to a self-fulfilling career, but to the general concept of balancing our time in worthwhile endeavors such as family, friends, and the community. Roosevelt added, "In any moment of decision, the best thing you can do is the right thing, the next best thing is the wrong thing, and the worst thing you can do is nothing."

Ironically, some lengthy time-management seminars can be a big waste of time. If one lacks time management skills, they can be learned and applied quickly. The eight rules of time management are:

1. *If you fail to plan, you plan to fail.* Poor planning not only causes many of the disasters that I study, it erodes valuable time in everyday lives. Lincoln said, "I do not think much of a man who is not wiser today than he was yesterday."

2. *Follow the advice of the Dalai Lama, who says, "Spend some time alone every day."* Fifteen minutes of planning increases efficiency 25 percent to 50 percent for the next twenty-four hours. When I get into the office each morning, I immediately sit down and plan out my day in writing. It is a simple process, but my day is far more productive for it.

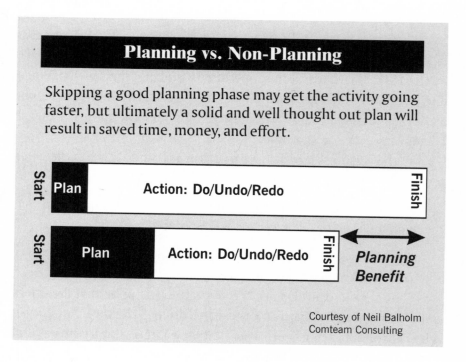

Planning vs. Non-Planning

Skipping a good planning phase may get the activity going faster, but ultimately a solid and well thought out plan will result in saved time, money, and effort.

Start | Plan | Action: Do/Undo/Redo | Finish

Start | Plan | Action: Do/Undo/Redo | Finish | ↔ *Planning Benefit*

Courtesy of Neil Balholm
Comteam Consulting

Daily Planning

Written daily plans are essential for anyone who has significant responsibilities. Nobody can be proactive all of the time. The skill in time management is having the sense of knowing when to be proactive and when to be reactive. A written plan, such as this, increases efficiency.

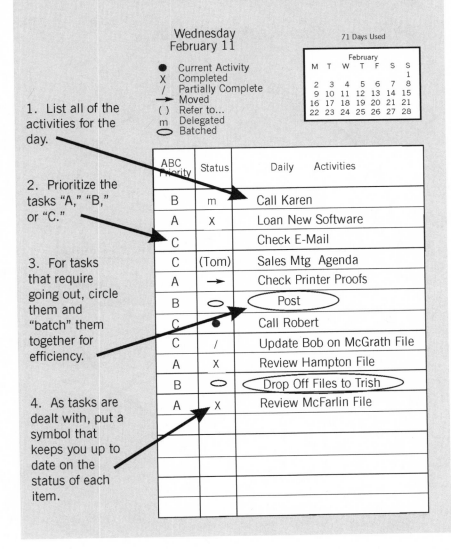

1. List all of the activities for the day.

2. Prioritize the tasks "A," "B," or "C."

3. For tasks that require going out, circle them and "batch" them together for efficiency.

4. As tasks are dealt with, put a symbol that keeps you up to date on the status of each item.

Wednesday
February 11

71 Days Used

- Current Activity
X Completed
/ Partially Complete
→ Moved
( ) Refer to...
m Delegated
⬭ Batched

February						
M	T	W	T	F	S	S
						1
2	3	4	5	6	7	8
9	10	11	12	13	14	15
16	17	18	19	20	21	21
22	23	24	25	26	27	28

ABC Priority	Status	Daily Activities
B	m	Call Karen
A	X	Loan New Software
C		Check E-Mail
C	(Tom)	Sales Mtg Agenda
A	→	Check Printer Proofs
B	⬭	Post
C	●	Call Robert
C	/	Update Bob on McGrath File
A	X	Review Hampton File
B	⬭	Drop Off Files to Trish
A	X	Review McFarlin File

Where Does My Time Go?

This chart gives you a better idea.

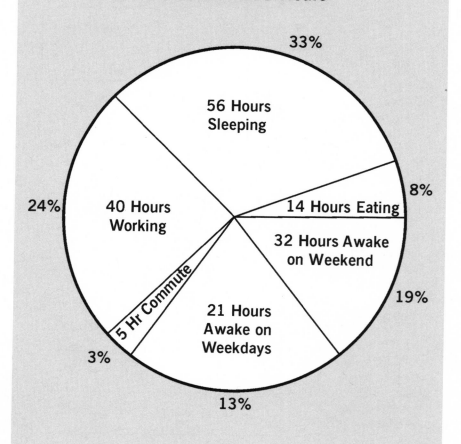

One Week - 168 Hours

33%

56 Hours
Sleeping

8%

14 Hours Eating

24%

40 Hours
Working

32 Hours Awake
on Weekend

19%

5 Hr Commute

21 Hours
Awake on
Weekdays

3%

13%

Time is Money

Time really is money. Unplanned disruptions can not only be annoying, but expensive. Knowing better just what our time is worth can help us use it more effectively.

How Much is Time Worth?

Year	Month	Week	Day	Hour	Minute
$ 15,000	$ 1,250	$ 288	$ 58	$ 7	$ 0.12
$ 20,000	$ 1,667	$ 385	$ 77	$ 10	$ 0.16
$ 25,000	$ 2,083	$ 481	$ 96	$ 12	$ 0.20
$ 30,000	$ 2,500	$ 577	$ 115	$ 14	$ 0.24
$ 40,000	$ 3,333	$ 769	$ 154	$ 19	$ 0.32
$ 50,000	$ 4,167	$ 962	$ 192	$ 24	$ 0.40
$ 60,000	$ 5,000	$ 1,154	$ 231	$ 29	$ 0.48
$ 75,000	$ 6,250	$ 1,442	$ 288	$ 36	$ 0.60
$ 100,000	$ 8,333	$ 1,923	$ 385	$ 48	$ 0.80
$ 125,000	$ 10,417	$ 2,404	$ 481	$ 60	$ 1.00
$ 150,000	$ 12,500	$ 2,885	$ 577	$ 72	$ 1.20
$ 175,000	$ 14,583	$ 3,365	$ 673	$ 84	$ 1.40
$ 200,000	$ 16,667	$ 3,846	$ 769	$ 96	$ 1.60

The 4 Quadrants

The 4 Quadrants is an outstanding time management tool developed by Stephen R. Covey, and incorporates President Dwight Eisenhower's concepts of importance and urgency.

Q1: Stress Quadrant
- Immediate priorities
- Induces crises, emergencies, imminent deadlines, urgent problems and so on
- These are fire drills that tend to cause stress and burnout
- Strategy: Do It Now!

Q2: Value Quadrant
- This are important issues, but not urgent
- Includes education, relationships, and long-term projects
- The most value is created in this quadrant
- Strategy: Calendar and Complete. These activities should be completed before they become urgent

Q3: Deception Quadrant
- These activities appears productive, but are not
- Includes most interruptions, many e-mails, unscheduled phone calls, and some poorly planned meetings
- Strategy: Delegate. Hand off these tasks or batch them together to address at a scheduled time

Q4: Regret Quadrant
- Neither important nor urgent
- Time passing activities, such as some phone calls, and too much television, video games, internet
- Essentially a waste of time and later regretted
- Strategy: Eliminate

Most people are Q1 and Q3 dominant. The "urgency" gives some people a rush, and a feeling that they are important; however, the objective is to spend as much time as possible in Q2. The more time invested in Q2, the less stress and need for urgency, and the greater satisfaction in knowing that important items are being addressed.

	Urgent	Not Urgent
Important	**QI** ACTIVITIES: Crises Pressing problems Deadline-driven projects	**QII** ACTIVITIES: Prevention Relationship building Recreation New opportunities
Not Important	**QIII** ACTIVITIES: Interruptions Some phone calls Some meetings Popular activities	**QIV** ACTIVITIES: Trivial Some mail Time wasters

Source: Dr. Stephen R. Covey, *First Things First*

3. *Use part of your planning time to write down the day's priorities.* Write down everything that you want to accomplish in your calendar. Remember that every time you think "I've got to remember . . ." it causes the same kind of stress as trying to wake up on time without an alarm clock. Writing things down relieves this stress.

4. *Prioritize your list of things to do.* Often the first thing you do sets the tone for the rest of the day. So, take the absolute "must do" items and place a dot or an "A" by them. Then, place a "B" by the items you would like to do and a "C by the things that are not a high priority. Additionally, I circle all the tasks that require a car, so that I can "bundle" these tasks into only one trip.

5. *Do the most unpleasant tasks first*, so that you don't drain your mental energy during the day worrying about them. Just do them and get them out of the way. As someone once said, "It's best to eat the biggest frog first."

SWOT Analysis

SWOT analysis is a useful technique used for understanding an organization's strategic position.

Strengths: The capabilities, resources and advantages of an organization.

Weaknesses: Things the organization is not good at, areas of resource scarcity and areas where the organization is vulnerable.

Opportunities: The good opportunities open to the organization, perhaps those that exploit its strengths or eliminate its weaknesses.

Threats: Things that can damage the organization, perhaps as people exploit its limitations or as its environment changes.

6. Items of personal "daily discipline," such as *exercise and reading something of significance, should not be placed on tomorrow's list.*

7. After setting the priorities, *get moving*. Remember, "The harder I work, the luckier I get." Success comes from putting priorities into action.

8. *As you accomplish the tasks on your list, check them off.* The physical action of checking off completed tasks is physiologically satisfying.

Being *Aggressive* Means Making Every Minute Count

David Copperfield is one of the most successful entertainers of all time. He has a star on the Hollywood Walk of Fame, has won more than twenty Grammy Awards, earned several Guinness World Records and is consistently listed as one of Forbes top money makers.

On one occasion, David called and invited my family to his show. We did and we loved it. After the show, David took my son Steven and me to his secret warehouse. David spent hours showing us huge stage props, storage rooms stacked to the ceiling with cases full of illusions, and he showed us his collection from past magicians, the largest such collection in the world. David showed Steven and me an incredible Houdini collection, including the famous Chinese Water Torture Cell, straight jackets, handcuffs and even Houdini's baby shoe! While this tour was amazing in many regards, one of the best moments was in the business offices.

We went into a room with thousands upon thousands of video tapes. I was surprised to learn that every single show was video-taped. I asked why, and was told that they wanted to note every un-choreographed moment, both good and bad. They labeled the good moments with a green dot, and any bad moments with a red dot. The "green dot" videos provided David with an invaluable source of great material for future shows, while the "red dot" mate-rial was reviewed to eliminate problems from reoccurring.

The process works. When I was in Las Vegas where the show was playing, I noted dozens of billboards for many performers; however, I hardly saw any for David Copperfield. David's producer told me that

Making Lists

Virtually no one can compete in today's complex society without a written plan. Business demands key organizational skills, and running a household is as complex or even more complex than many business operations.

Simply making lists, and then prioritizing those lists is an accumulation of numerous desirable traits.

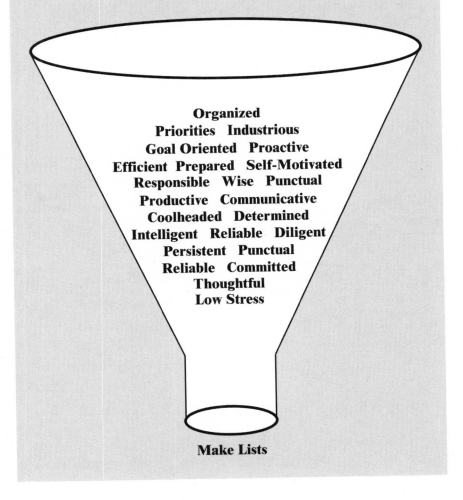

Organized
Priorities   Industrious
Goal Oriented   Proactive
Efficient Prepared   Self-Motivated
Responsible Wise   Punctual
Productive   Communicative
Coolheaded   Determined
Intelligent   Reliable   Diligent
Persistent   Punctual
Reliable   Committed
Thoughtful
Low Stress

Make Lists

Meeting Agenda

Written meeting agendas are a "must" and are the responsibility of the person in charge. A form such as this sets a clear objective and facilitates each of the agenda items. All meetings should have a start time and an ending time. The leader has a responsibility to keep things on track.

Meeting Agenda

1. List date, time, and place

2. Set a specific purpose for the meeting

3. List roles for the team leader, meeting facilitator, recorder, and list the participants

4. List any special objectives or notes

5. List each agenda item, the person in charge for that item, and a specific time for each item

6. List the decided action for each item

Date: 5-15   Time: 9:30 am   Place: Office

Purpose of Meeting: Set Pricing of New Product

Leader: Kathy

Facilitator: Peter

Recorder: Mike

Participants: Kathy, Peter, Mike, Sam Lishman, Ashley, Abe, Orell, Donna

Special Notes: We must have a price set by the end of the meeting.

Agenda Item:	Time	Decided Action:	Person In Charge:
Objectives	15	- - -	Kathy
Costs	10	Min 2x cost	Peter
Competition	30	Can be higher	Donna
Customers	20	Low sensitivity	Abe, Orell
Decision	15	Set at $15.95	Peter

Operations Worksheet

Even a small project requires written coordination. A sheet such as this can keep track of each activity, who is responsible, and the key dates.

Operations Worksheet

1. List the project

2. List key people involved

3. List each task required by the group

4. Set key dates

5. List team member who is responsible for each task

Project:	Test Winsharr Product	
Contacts:	Mark, Paul, Barbara, Bobbie	
Key Date:	Activity:	Team Member:
11-17	Get prototype	Barbara
11-30	Duplicate 10 copies	Mark
12-3	Install at test sites	Mark, Paul
12-5	Train test site users	Bobbie
1-15	Monitor use, report	Paul, Barbara
2-1	Compile feedback	Bobbie
2-15	Formal report	Paul

David's show is so stellar, that they simply do not have to advertise as much, but that the theaters are always full.

This provided a glimpse into the mindset required to the very highest levels of achievement. David Copperfield did not just wander aimlessly into success, but rather he literally recorded every moment on stage so that he could review and perfect his performances. When he has an unplanned bright moment, he takes note and adds it to future shows. When there is a problem, he does not bury his head in the sand. He directly faces it, carefully reviews and fixes the problem. Through this building process, he has reached the very highest levels of success in the entertainment field.

I have spent years observing the traits of those who are highly effective in both crisis and stable periods. They invariably have ten operational mindsets that show a high degree of respect for their time:

1. *The Future.* All of life will be spent in the future. They know that action is a requirement, or they will spend their lives simply react-ing. Achievers learn from the past, but their eyes are on the future.

2. *Time is Life.* Most people would never consider self-destruction or suicide, yet some throw away their lives in many wasted minutes and hours. For achievers, "time" is considered a precious com-modity that is jealously guarded. It is thought of in terms of min-utes and hours rather than in terms of days, weeks, or months.

3. *Crave a Challenge.* Achievers avoid boredom. They crave a chal-lenge as they know boredom leads to stress and ineffective lives.

4. *Pause and Plan.* Days simply go better when a few minutes are spent planning them out.

5. *Identify the Priority.* The hallmark of achievement is to focus and handle the top priority. With no priorities, a person or organiza-tion becomes a closed system where there is a flurry of activity but nothing is done with any real benefit.

6. *Focus.* Achievers aim at the big prize, and let the small ones go to others. *There is never time to do everything that there is to do.* Success is a matter of setting priorities and focusing on them. Achievers

have a clear focus on what they have to do vs. what they want to do. They have a single-minded, focused concentration on the key goal. They never "major in minors" or spend time in the easy, quick, ineffective activities.

7. *Discipline*. Achievers make a habit of doing things that the non-achiever will not do.

8. *Delineate*. Creative and administrative tasks are incompatible. They need to be delineated into different parts of the day.

9. *Quality*. Achievers know the old saying, "There is never enough time to do it right, but always enough time to do it over."

10. *Lists*. Achievers are chronic "list makers" and never feel too busy to make a list. Every focused, successful, effective person makes lists.

11. *Meetings*. An achiever is always considerate of others and will have a clear, written agenda for every meeting. Of course, they will keep the discussion on track and dismiss the meeting on time.

Operational Lessons

- Success is putting priorities into action.
- Productive daily operations must be preserved at all costs.
- Even the biggest task will get completed if tackled just a step at a time.
- The time to repair the roof is when the sun is shining
- Choose your battles. Being "proactive" on all fronts is an unreasonable demand.
- "No comment" is translated by many to mean, "I'm guilty." Always make some comment when challenged.
- The best thing about the future is that it only comes one day at a time.
- Remember, "If you fail to plan, you plan to fail."
- Procrastination only makes a small problem bigger. Ask, "If I don't have time to do it now, when can I do it?"
- Spend some time alone every day and plan out your time. This will increase your productivity substantially.
- Write down everything you want to accomplish and then prioritize.
- "Eat the biggest frog first." Do your most unpleasant tasks first; then you are set free to focus on more enjoyable tasks.
- "The harder I work, the luckier I get."
- Identify and avoid the activities that will waste your time.
- Say "no" to unreasonable and wasteful requests or invitations.
- Time is a precious resource. People of value know this and always carefully choose where to use it.
- As actions are accomplished, give yourself credit and check them off.

Chapter Ten

Consequential

Leave a Legacy

When I was a kid, my dad gave me some advice I'll never forget. He said that whenever I was faced with a big decision, I should think ahead five or ten years and ask myself if I would look back and be proud of that decision or not.

That was good advice. Whether one likes it or not, everyone ultimately owns their past activities. Everyone, every day is building a legacy, a reputation by which they will be thought of, and this legacy will determine their opportunities for the future as well as those around them.

I have an interest in my family's legacy. The Bells come from the large Bell clan of Scotland. Some of the family moved from Scotland and my seventh great-grandfather was born in 1627 in York, England. His son, Shadrack Bell immigrated to New Hampshire soon after the Mayflower landed. His son Thomas colonized in North Carolina. His son Robert was a lieutenant in the Revolutionary War, and his son, William, my third great-grandfather, fought in the Revolutionary War as a private and later established a large plantation in Tennessee that still stands to this day. William's son Alfred moved to Illinois, and later was an early pioneer and moved west. His son Eli, my great-grandfather, lived in Hawaii and supervised the building of the first sugar mill there. His son, my grandfather Milton Oliver, was very industrious and built and owned seven homes in California. The Depression wiped out three of them, but he kept going. My dad graduated from UCLA and later headed up research and development at Fender Guitars. He and

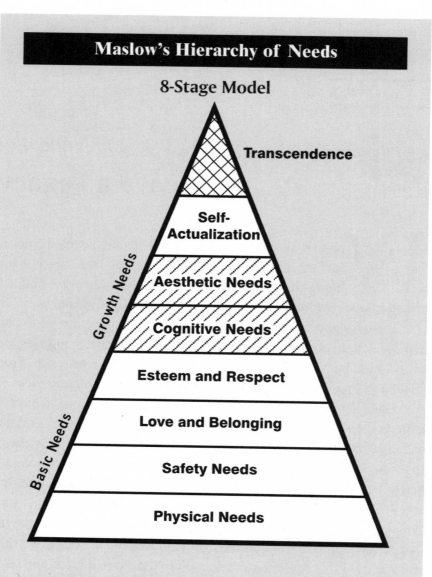

In the 1990s, Maslow's Hierarchy of Needs was modified by some to include a new pinnacle category, "Transcendence Needs," or the need to help others reach self-actualization. Building a legacy includes helping others in both their basic and growth needs.

my mom have spent a total of four and a half years of their lives living with and helping the underprivileged in Mexico, Ecuador, and Peru.

That's the Bells. My other third great-grandfather, John M. Bernhisel, was a doctor from New York who later served five terms in the U.S. Congress. He met regularly with Presidents Fillmore, Pierce, and Lincoln. To top this legacy off, my uncle directed many Hollywood movies and later was a director of Gilligan's Island!

I think that the best way to get a perspective on life is to study the legacy of others, particularly our own family members and ancestors. Their experiences can be inspiring. A good way to honor our ancestors is to remember them, while the best way is to try and build upon what they have done. I have read the histories and journals of many of my ancestors, and it strikes me that none of them thought that they were doing much of anything remarkable. In their minds, they were just taking the challenges as they came along and doing their best.

Those who do not have a great heritage have a particularly great opportunity to learn from the mistakes of the past, put an end to them and put their lives on an upward trajectory. One can learn just as much from a bad example as a good example.

History is not just fascinating, but it contains a wealth of information that can be applicable today. As we examine past crises, actions, reactions, and results, we get valuable insights into today's challenges.

For many years, those of us who are in the business have known of three lingering major threats to America. Specifically, these are: a major terrorist attack (probably in New York City), a major California earthquake, and a collapse of the levy system in New Orleans. Of course, the terrorist attacks became a reality on September 11, and the California earthquake is yet to happen, but on August 29, 2005, the levy system did collapse in New Orleans.

The broken levies allowed millions of gallons of water to spill into vast areas of New Orleans, flooding thousands of homes and businesses up to ten feet or more. The hurricane winds ripped apart roofs, and later spun off into tornadoes that did further damage. The thirty-five-foot

Weeks after the water subsided, damage from Hurricane Katrina was still over-whelming, going on for miles and miles.

A ship had floated over the levee and ended up right in the middle of the street.

storm surge came into the Mississippi coast like a freight train that created tsunami-like destruction up to fifteen miles inland.

It is safe to say that I have inspected every major disaster site in the United States and many others around the world, but I have never seen such widespread damage as I saw in the aftermath of Hurricane Katrina. I have seen many destroyed neighborhoods, but never a site where the damage went on mile after mile, for about seventy miles! Every house, church, business, and store was blown apart or simply gone altogether. Many of the New Orleans downtown high-rise buildings were skeletons with their windows blown out.

The damage was so vast, that months after the hurricane, many areas had hardly been touched, much less restored. Of course, there has been widespread discussion of how—or if—to rebuild New Orleans and the Mississippi Gulf Coast. From a managerial standpoint, it simply does not make sense to rebuild in the same way in an area where these same risks still exist. I believe that the Gulf Coast must have a buffer zone along the coast where only blow-through designs (like in the tsunami zones of Hilo, Hawaii) are permitted. Furthermore, I believe that some areas of New Orleans should simply not be rebuilt. It makes far better sense to spend the rebuilding dollars in areas that are fundamentally not at risk and that never should have been built in the first place. In business and life, we must incorporate the lessons into our strategies for going forward.

Some build remarkable legacies; others do little of value, while still others leave a poor legacy. But some legacies are so bad that their only value is to be a warning to others.

The World's Worst Legacy

Of all of the disasters I have researched, I'm often asked which one was the worst.

The answer is simple: Auschwitz. It has always been interesting to me that the world's worst disaster was not caused by tornadoes, earthquakes, tsunamis, or floods, but by bigotry, intolerance, and hatred.

Millions of people came down these railroad tracks
to the horrible Nazi death camps.

My visit to the concentration camps in Poland had a profound impact on me. I was absolutely stunned at the grand scale of this operation. There were row upon row of wooden barracks, long rows of wooden toilet seats and miles of barbed-wire fencing. The camp was so large that even from the top of a guard tower, I couldn't see it all. And this was only *one* of dozens of concentration camps.

I was sickened as I stood by myself in the gas chambers and thought about the atrocities. No words can really explain these feelings of horror. I walked among the trees where women and children were forced to wait their turn for the gas chambers while ashes from the crematoriums fell on them like rain. I walked along the railroad tracks that led into Berkinau.

Denial Isn't Going to Teach Us Anything

The events perpetrated by the Nazis were beyond horrific, and it's easy to see why many people avoided talking about them then and even now. I admire the people who work there to preserve these camps and document the events so that the world will not lose the valuable lessons. As encouraging as that is, at the time I was there, so-called "ethnic cleansing" was occurring in Kosovo. With such a

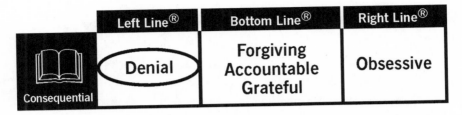

	Left Line®	Bottom Line®	Right Line®
Consequential	**Denial**	**Forgiving Accountable Grateful**	**Obsessive**

horrible event in our world history to learn from, I had to ask myself, "Did we really learn our lessons here?"

It's one thing to have a tragedy, but it is another to repeat it.

Big or small, a forgotten lesson erodes a valuable problem-solving skill. Auschwitz teaches us that we should never forget the lessons of the past. Ever.

Obsessive **Behavior Is Not Any Better Than Being in Denial**

The tragedies in Waco, Texas, on April 19, 1993, clearly point to an example of stepping over the Right Line into obsessiveness. After an initial raid in February, the U.S. government returned that April morning with tanks, armored vehicles, and chemical weapons. At day's end, more than one hundred men, women, and children had died.

When I visited Waco, I met several people who had known David Koresh, the leader of the Branch Davidians. Though he could be labeled a "cultist," he often went into town and even visited some of the local nightclubs. He was hardly a hermit and clearly did not behave at all like a fugitive. Koresh was on amicable terms with the local sheriff. He could have been easily arrested or questioned during one of his frequent visits into town. Many people believe that, even if a simple phone call had been allowed between the sheriff and Koresh, the FBI's raid might not have occurred at *all*.

We will never know because these more sensible tactics were never attempted. Instead, strong-arm Right Line tactics sent tanks into a house occupied by small children and mothers.

The results of an overbearing assault are really brought home for those who visit the site. Certainly, the Branch Davidians marched to the beat of a different drummer, but the government went out of bounds in dealing with them. At the site, you'll find a tree planted in memory of every person who died that day. Many of the granite markers are for small babies who were just a few months old. I walked around the underground tunnels at the site and saw the belongings of the children who had once lived there and what the fire had done.

Amazingly, Janet Reno and law enforcement officials refused to acknowledge their mistakes at Waco, instead insisting on "explaining" their decision to invade a residence full of little children with fire-throwing tanks. This lack of acknowledgment is a key sign of excessive behavior, where the leaders failed, and then failed again to acknowledge it.

Reno was so oblivious to her own incompetence that she even ran for political office. But it came as no surprise to the rest of us when she lost. Hopefully, others have paid attention to the inept decisions made in Waco and have learned the lesson.

Forgiveness Is a Key Attribute of Achievement

Forgiveness is the ability to completely let go of anger and resentment towards another person or organization.

In practical terms, it is always easier to forgive someone who apologizes and, where applicable, pays restitution. Certainly, if someone has

The Waco Site Today

done something wrong, sincerely apologizes, and does whatever they can to correct the situation, then we have a duty to accept the apology and not harbor resentment. Likewise, when we have done something wrong ourselves, we cannot really move forward without first apologizing and doing whatever is necessary to repair the situation.

However, sometimes we are faced with situations where there has been an offence or crime, and the offender lacks the character and ethics to apologize. They may in fact be an everyday sociopath-one who simply goes through life without any real conscience and who is "past feeling." The situation may be improved somewhat if the perpetrator is caught, reprimanded, demoted, fired, or imprisoned. However, even for the worst offences, a perpetrator may never get caught or apologize, and justice may never be served. These are the hardest situations for forgiveness.

While it is difficult, it still must be done. One cannot have healthy lives or build new relationships without getting past the upsets of the past. Not forgiving keeps us in the struggle. We must move effectively through the "Five Stages of Grief," those being Denial, Anger, Bargaining, Depression, and Acceptance. Only upon finally accepting things the way they are, can we then move on to achievement.

To forgive, the first step is to dismiss some notions, such as "forgive and forget." While that makes sense with lots of life's daily bumps and bruises, no reasonable person could "forget" a murder, abusive behavior, or other serious situation. While time can play a major role in dulling the pain, there are simply some conditions that cannot successfully be forgotten. In fact, some psychologist say that "premature forgiveness" damages the subconscious mind, and that one cannot forgive until they have fully felt the pain that has been caused.

Nor does forgiveness mean "acceptance." Indeed, the greatest misconception about forgiveness is that we are required to somehow reconcile with the perpetrator. Forgiveness should not be confused with reconciliation. No rational, kind, and forgiving person could ever accept or condone the atrocities of the Holocaust, September 11, child abuse, or other horrible event. We may very well need to

Mindset

"Nothing is Neutral"

Some people dwell on problems, while others immediately look for solutions. Those with a solution mindset will always prevail over those who are drawn to chaos and problems.

		Problem Mindset	Solution Mindset
PURPOSE	Philosophical	Lack of Direction Denial	"Know Thyself" Take Responsibility - Passion Focus - Gratitude - Flexible - Trust
	Intellectual	Action Before Thinking	Think Before You Act Read, Read, Read Chronically Take Notes
PEOPLE	Sociological	Lack of Defined Roles or Responsibilities	Associate with Achievers Create Barriers to the Competition
	Influential	Indecisive Worry of Hurting Feelings Blame Poor Human Relations	Love for the "Customer" Always Thinking "Marketing" Open-Door Policy Laughter Improves Performance
PRODUCTIVITY	Physical	Neglect Poor Product Quality	Stay Fit Product and Services Are Well Suited for the Market
	Environmental	Clutter Poor Maintenance	Respect the Environment Enjoy Art
	Financial	Get Rich Schemes No Budget - Impatient Greed - Poor Cost Control	Choose Work That You Enjoy Spend Less Than You Earn
PROGRESS	Developmental	Reactive vs. Active Lack of Written Goals Failure to Look at Trends	Written Goals and Plans Tools: Brainstorming, Negotiation, Mind Mapping, Decision Making
	Operational	No Lists No Calendar No Priorities	Pause to Plan Every Day Lists, Lists, Lists "Time Is Life"
	Consequential	No Legacy	A Life Worth Living Is Worth Recording

distance ourselves from someone who has ongoing toxic behavior, and in some cases, we have every right and responsibility to do so. Forgiveness does not mean having to waive our legal rights.

To forgive, we must first dispel the myths.

Forgiveness does not require forgetting, acceptance of bad behavior, or reconciliation.

The word "forgiveness" is built on the root word "give." The key of forgiveness is that it is a choice we make to benefit ourselves, not so much the offender. Indeed, no one benefits from forgiveness more than the one who forgives. While you may "give" the offender the release of your hatred or fury, more importantly you "give" yourself the ability to let go of negative feelings and move on.

Anger and resentment are like a ball and chain locked onto our ankle, keeping us from where we want to go. The choice to not forgive means remaining angry, resentful, bitter, vindictive, and miserable. To forgive, we could ask ourselves some questions, "Do I let go and move ahead with my life or do I spend my time stuck where I am and consumed by somebody else's bad behavior?" Or, in other words, "Does my desire to do something positive for myself and those I love outweigh my hatred and anger," or "Are my time, energy, and emotional health worth wasting on this situation?" One political leader, pointing at chronic wars between two groups stated that the conflicts could only end when both parties decided to love their own children more than they hated each other.

Forgiveness is an internal outlook on people, situations, and life. Robert Enright, a developmental psychologist at the University of Wisconsin says it this way:

Forgiveness is giving up the resentment to which you are entitled and offering to the person who hurt you friendlier attitudes to which they are not entitled.

Forgiving people are at peace with themselves. They let small stuff go altogether. They are not easily offended. They forget about the guy that cut them off in traffic. They are courteous to those who may not deserve it, like the police officer who treats a suspect firmly but courteously as they place them in the squad car, the parent who finds out that their child who has done something wrong, but hugs them anyway, or the boss who must correct a subordinate, and then invites him or her to a baseball game.

For some situations, forgiveness may take considerable time, and it may come in steps, but once we make that choice to forgive, we can let go of a host of negative conditions and direct our attention to healing and being positive and productive. Reverend Karyl Huntley said, "You know you have forgiven someone when he or she has harmless passage through your mind."

Science has even recognized the benefits of forgiveness, which has been linked to helping chronic back pain, easing depression, and reducing stress levels. Forgiveness is one of the key coping mechanisms that even helps those who are ill to heal quicker and can even help those who are terminally ill to live longer or better quality lives. In all its forms, letting go allows us go move forward.

Being *Accountable* Means Doing Our Duty . . . No Matter What

Accountability is taking ownership for one's actions. Philosophy, principles, and plans must be "owned" to be real. Accountability requires clear expectations that are consistent with the philosophy and values of the organization. To be "accountable" means that one must accept one's responsibilities along with the result of one's actions, good or bad. Accountable people, once they have studied a situation and have made a commitment, are unshakable.

As a little boy, I always heard the phrase, "Remember the Alamo!" I knew that it had something to do with a battle in Texas, but that was the extent of my knowledge. Once I gave a lecture in San Antonio, and I finally had the opportunity to visit the Alamo. I imagined that it would be in some remote part of the desert, but it was actually right outside of my downtown hotel, so I set aside a day to visit.

The Alamo

It wasn't until that day that I learned that the Texans held their ground to defend their fort and, in so doing, all of them were killed. Frankly, *I was surprised to learn that the "good guys" lost the battle.*

Initially, I wondered why anyone would go out of his or her way to remember *that* kind of lesson. But I learned that these men remained accountable to their commitments, no matter what the consequences were. While standing their ground, these brave men inflicted such great losses on the Mexican Army that the Mexicans were defeated just a few weeks later. *I realized, then, that even a loss can be a positive lesson and motivator.*

The Texan forces had made a commitment to defend their fort, and they were uniquely brave. Even though greatly outnumbered and defeated, they fought hard and gave their lives rather than surrender. Those who won the war felt accountable to the great men who had preceded them at the Alamo.

Yes, they lost the battle, but because of their efforts the war was won.

Of the fifty traits outlined in the Global Matrix, "Accountability" is the most important. In a world where blame and wining is the status quo, responsibility is paramount to success. This concept is so powerful that there is even a movement to build a "Statue of Responsibility" on the West Coast as a "bookend" to the Statue of Liberty on the East Coast. The concept is based on Dr. Viktor E. Frankl's concept that:

Liberty + Responsibility = Freedom

Nations, organizations, businesses, and people who take responsibility for their behavior—rather than playing the old blame game—are inevitably the highest achievers.

Even in the Worst Situations, There's Something to Be *Grateful* For

Everyone will remember where he or she was on the morning of September 11, 2001.

I was at home preparing to leave for my office when the phone rang. My wife was taking our daughter and her friend to kindergarten, and her friend's parents had heard the news. My wife called and told me that terrorists had hijacked and crashed planes into the World Trade Center and the Pentagon . . . another jet had crashed in Pennsylvania . . . and that the entire World Trade Center had collapsed!

I was in shock.

I turned on the television and saw the unthinkable play and replay. My day's plans were forgotten. Throughout the entire civilized world, everyday life came to an abrupt standstill.

My home phone rang, and it was a reporter from the *London Times*. She wanted my comments, which were printed in the next day's paper.

This was a horrific act with ramifications like no other. Like most businesspeople, I thought, "That could have been me." I flew on American Airlines through Newark all the time. On trips to New York, I would often go to the observation decks at the World Trade Center.

I knew that we would never "get over" something of this magnitude, but our nation's history has proven that we would eventually get through it.

On a practical level, I had an immediate choice to make. I had speaking and business engagements in New York in just a few days. I had to decide whether to go or cancel my trip. My initial inclination

The Skeleton of the World Trade Center

As I walked down the street by the WTC, I had just stepped on a manhole cover, and it burst into flames. The firemen came immediately to put out the underground fire.

231

The New York City landscape prior to September 11th.

was to cancel everything. I called my airline, and to my surprise, my flights were still scheduled. My clients told me that coming would help people get back into life and move ahead. Still completely overwhelmed, I flew out to New York about a week later.

As my plane made its final approach to Newark Airport, we flew parallel to Manhattan Island. I could see floodlights around the disaster area and the smoke still billowing out. It was a sickening sight. You could have heard a pin drop on the plane as we all looked on in horror.

After giving my lecture, I took the subway down to "ground zero." Although I had seen plenty of pictures in the media, nothing could have prepared me for the disaster in front of me. I simply could not believe what my eyes were seeing. Skeletons of the lower World Trade Center buildings still leaned askew, and piles of rubble loomed in such a huge, vast area that words and photos couldn't possibly describe the scene. The smoke was still surging from the rubble. In fact, as I stood there, a manhole I was standing on erupted in flames. As I ran, the smoke engulfed me and the emergency workers nearby.

Later I walked by the fire stations of the lost fire fighters, and was haunted by the numerous hand-made "missing posters" plastered everywhere. I am still stunned by this catastrophe.

This temporary memorial for Flight 93 was used by President Bush and the heroes' families and sits near the point of the jet's impact.

Like any disaster, it exposed the true character of those it impacted. It not only affected the United States, but the entire freedom-loving world. As awful and unthinkable as the disaster was, so was the overwhelming and uniting effect of its aftermath.

The World Trade Center damages, as estimated by the New York City Mayor's Office, were staggering.

- Clean up and stabilization of the WTC site: $9.0 billion
- Repairing and replacing damaged infrastructure: $9.0 billion
- Rebuilding the World Trade Center, as smaller buildings: $6.7 billion
- Repairing and restoring other damaged buildings: $5.3 billion
- Lost rents of the destroyed buildings: $1.75 billion

The Terrorist Attacks on September 11 Could Have Been Much Worse

Later, the city and state of New York retained me to compute the economic damages to the World Trade Center site. In the process, I learned a lot that the media did not report. While there has been a great deal spoken about this horrible tragedy—and indeed the damage is hardly imaginable—there was *more*, actually, to be grateful for.

Consider the following:
- The World Trade Center is not just the two towers, but also a complex of seven buildings where more than 50,000 people work.
- The Marriott Hotel was completely destroyed, and several others were damaged. More than 12.5 million square feet of New York "Class A" office space was destroyed, and 13.3 million square feet were damaged.
- More than 110,000 people visited this complex on a typical business day.
- The falling debris and smoke was so thick that it could have been fatal to thousands of others who were fleeing blocks away.
- On that morning, a two-car accident in the Holland Tunnel blocked traffic and prevented thousands from getting to work on time at the World Trade Center.
- While, sadly, more than 3,000 people lost their lives, at least 45,000 successfully escaped, were rescued, or were late to work because of the traffic.
- Approximately 23,000 people work at the Pentagon. Of that, 123 lost their lives. That is an amazing 99.5 percent survival rate.
- The two American Airlines and the two United flights were approximately three-quarters *empty*. As any business traveler knows, it is unusual that there were so many empty seats out of Newark and Boston on a business morning.
- United Flight 93 passengers fought the terrorists and thwarted a fourth attack, saving untold lives.

The hijacked planes were largely empty. The Pentagon attack was largely unsuccessful. The overwhelming majority of people in the World Trade Center buildings escaped. A devoted group of passengers gave the ultimate sacrifice to save even more lives.

Even in the aftermath of this horrible tragedy, there are many things to be grateful for. Out of more than 100,000 people who were directly targeted by the terrorists, well over 97 percent escaped, survived, or otherwise avoided the attacks.

The O. J. Simpson Case: An Array of Lessons

The O. J. Simpson case is another example of a bright side coming from one of the saddest of situations. *The prosecution had a wealth of evidence against Simpson:*

- A long history of abuse by Simpson already existed.
- A bloody glove was left at the crime scene matching one found at Simpson's estate.
- The victims' blood was in his white Ford Bronco.
- The blood on the gloves matched both the victims.
- Simpson had sustained an injury on his hand, and his blood was found at the crime scene.
- A trail of blood led up Simpson's driveway and into his house.
- Simpson's houseguest, Brian "Kato" Kaelin, had heard someone walking along the side of the house, exactly where the matching glove had been found.
- Footprints at the crime scene matched Simpson's foot size.
- Even more bizarre, when Simpson's arrest was imminent, he left a rambling note and took cash, his passport, and a disguise and fled the area. He was later found, and the entire city of Los Angeles nearly shut down to watch a strange, low-speed chase as Simpson's friend drove him back to the Rockingham estate.

The evidence against Simpson was overwhelming.

Nevertheless, led by Marcia Clark, the prosecution committed blunder after blunder:

The Bundy Crime Scene from the Air

The prosecution asked Simpson to try on the leather glove with an unneeded latex glove already on his hand. Further, the leather glove had gotten moist with the blood, and the leather had shrunk.

- Simpson's attorneys—knowing that Simpson had flunked a lie detector test—were not about to let him testify, and Simpson took advantage of his right to not testify, but when Simpson tried on the glove, he was given a chance to *silently* testify as he "struggled" with the glove.
- Blood preservatives were found in some blood samples without explanation, casting doubt on the integrity of some of the evidence.
- Remarkably, despite the high profile of this case, Detective Phillip Vannatter and Detective Tom Lange neglected to investigate numerous key facts that had been first reported to them by Detective Mark Fuhrman. For example, an empty Swiss Army knife box found in Simpson's bathroom was not collected as evidence.
- Fuhrman had also found a bloody fingerprint on the gate at the rear of Nicole's walkway that was completely neglected by

The Front Door and Walkway at the Bundy Crime Scene

Vannatter and Lange. *That one item of evidence alone could have put Simpson away immediately.*

- With few places to go with the evidence, the "Dream Team" defense shifted the focus to Mark Fuhrman, who was portrayed as a racist. Nobody countered this attack. In fact, the prosecution went along with it and allowed the defense to shift the focus of the trial from O. J. himself.

- Fuhrman actually testified that he had never "addressed anyone" with a racist term. He never testified that he had not used the term, but again the prosecution never pointed out this distinction and did nothing to defend or rehabilitate him as a witness.

- The defense's strategy was intended to first cast what doubt they could on the physical evidence, while playing the "race card"—from the bottom of the deck.

- Finally, the "Dream Team" defense was successful in assembling twelve ignorant people on the jury.

Even the Judge Messed Up

Until that time, Judge Lance Ito had been respected in legal circles, but his decision to broadcast the trial was later criticized as the lawyers played to the cameras, creating a spectacle and grandstanding.

But it was worse than that. Behind the scenes, Ito's wife, police Captain Margaret York, had been Mark Fuhrman's supervisor, yet she signed a statement that she had no specific recollection of working with him. Many now believe that Ito's wife actually had *many* interactions with Fuhrman and thus perjured herself in order to allow her husband to preside over the high-profile case. Many believe that the defense knew this and constantly held it over Ito's head to squeeze him for favorable rulings.

Ito lost control of the courtroom. After a one-and-a-half year trial, and in a highly controversial verdict, Simpson was found "not guilty."

Later, in another more honorable courtroom, Simpson was subsequently found to be "responsible" for the deaths and ordered to pay $33.5 million in compensation to Nicole's children and the Goldman families. Simpson also lost his estate located on Rockingham Drive in Brentwood.

When a Media Case Strikes Home . . .

I was involved in measuring the economic impact that the crime stigma had on the Bundy property where the murder took place. Until my involvement, my experiences were largely the same as the rest of America: I considered it a hyped media event.

Then I went through the condominium, and I saw all the things I had heard about in the news. Nicole's candles were still by the bathtub. I saw the ring left by her ice cream cup on a ledge by the garage; I stood on the spot on the front patio where police believe that Simpson hid and spied through the window. I walked the walkway itself where the murders occurred. I stood by the tree stump where Ron Goldman's body was found.

That's when the reality of the event began to hit me.

Full Cycle - The End Depends Upon the Beginning

Each of these ten elements has an evolving effect on the other. The foundation of all people and organizations is the philosophical mindset and the organization's culture.

These philosophies eventually produce results, and those results themselves can then circle back and alter and influence our philosophies.

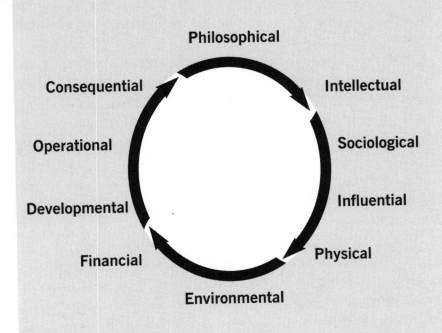

On one occasion, I went by the office of Nicole's father, Lou Brown, to drop off some paperwork. I had my daughter with me who, at the time, was a year old. My intention was to simply drop off the package at the reception area. Lou happened to be there, and he asked me to stay a few minutes.

Lou Brown is a great guy, a very kind man and a grandfatherly figure. He really had no interest in talking to me—he wanted to talk to and hold my beautiful little daughter. As Lou held her, I was jolted into a sobering perspective of this whole event.

As he played with my daughter and made her laugh, I got a small glimpse into his horrible loss. He was holding my little girl, but he had lost his. At that moment, the event went from a media circus to a horrible tragedy.

Losing a daughter or sister under such circumstances must have been an unbearable experience for the Brown family. The jury verdict in the criminal trial added to this devastation. In fact, the Brown family had been dealt a triple blow.

First, their daughter and sister had been murdered. Second, the man that the civil court found responsible was free. Third, a battle ensued over the custody of Nicole's two small children. In what many view as an inept ruling by Judge Nancy Wieben Stock, Simpson was given custody of his two young children, whom many feared he would use to shield himself from an angry public. The appellate court strongly ridiculed Judge Stock's decision and later overturned that judgment, but much of the damage was done. In 2000, Simpson was granted custody of the children.

Many people would have been irreparably crushed by such a set of circumstances. Remarkably, in spite of these horrible experiences and setbacks, the Browns channeled their anger, grief, and frustration into a positive effort by founding the Nicole Brown Charitable Foundation, which raises funds to assist women who are victims of domestic abuse. Nicole's sister, Denise and other members of the family have used the media attention from this event to increase the public's awareness of spousal abuse. As a result, many abused women have been helped at a time that might otherwise seem hopeless.

The O. J. Simpson case, like so many tragedies, shows *all* sides of human behavior. Problems are usually caused by behavior that is out of bounds, by either being Left Line, like the LAPD, Lance Ito, and the prosecution; or by the Right Line obsessiveness of O. J.

On the other hand, a crisis can bring out the best Bottom Line activity—as it did in the Brown family. Those who are most successful seem to inherently know that the hardest steel goes through the hottest fire.

A Global Approach to Achievement

One of our family mottos is, *Leave things better than we found them.*

I believe that the single most important question that people and organizations can ask themselves is *have we left things better than we found them?*

Indeed, the key to productivity and building a legacy is to always improve the current conditions. This means being encouraging, providing service, cleaning up messes—both tangible and intangible—and educating ourselves while helping others.

This can take many forms, from cheering up a store clerk or a fellow worker who is not having their best day, to raising kids who are happy and productive, to spending years with a business to help it run more productively. If we approach each situation that comes our way with the attitude that we are going to leave it better than we found it, we will inherently create a great legacy.

Building a legacy also demands that we understand that life is a test. We must start where we are and then build on that. To ultimately pass this test, we must appreciate and enjoy all of the good things, while also knowing that hurdles are going to be thrown our way. Those who are genuinely successful know that it is inevitable that problems are a part of every life's and every organization's landscape. Nobody has ever built a great legacy by avoiding problems. Anyone who has built a noteworthy legacy did so by facing the challenges and overcoming them.

Organizations must maneuver and work to remain viable in a world that is increasingly cluttered and competing for attention. Efficiency must be continuously monitored and improved upon. Attention must always be paid to the people in the organization in such a way that they not only want to stay, but that they have the resources and desire to be constructive.

Businesses will have to meet the challenges of competition, continuous research and training, quality control, deadlines, efficient production, building relationships, and keeping clients, customers, and employees both productive and happy.

Parents face the challenges of raising good children in a world full of risk, keeping impossible schedules, continually teaching, paying all the endless costs to keeping a household running, and—amongst all of this—putting in the time together as a family.

Achievement takes work. There is no honor for the timid or those who had everything handed to them. Nobody can build a legacy by avoiding and circumventing problems. There is no greatness in just doing the same old thing the way it has always been done. To build a genuine legacy, we must improve upon the status quo, take the challenges, and then conquer them. The harder the test, the greater the joy in passing it.

A positive attitude does not mean we get suckered into the self-absorbed and delusional notions that we think we're important because some "success guru" says we are, or doing jumping jacks while chanting that we can do anything. A positive attitude is grounded in the reality that we must take full responsibility for our lives and decisions and—while being grateful for what we have—taking the steps to reach even higher levels. And while reaching for more is good, it must be done in balance. We should not develop new products without also investing in our marketing efforts to promote them. It makes no sense to make more money while neglecting our family. In the same way, it is a poor choice to go on a family vacation when our finances are not in order. We must balance our efforts and elevate everything together.

From bigger challenges, we see some even bigger lessons. We see from even a horrible tragedy that there is *always* something to be grateful for. We see that no matter what, we must preserve the lessons. We see the value of channeling our grief into a worthwhile cause.

Personally, I have no more interest in a crisis then the average person who watches the evening news. My fascination comes from observing the level of thinking that caused the problem in the first place, and then watching how the situation is managed. I love the challenge of working through these complex problems. Evaluating all of the elements, we see that the "consequential" lessons ultimately come full circle and have an impact on the philosophical issues where everything begins.

As the saying goes, "The end depends upon the beginning."

Problems produce lessons . . .

Lessons produce value . . .

Value produces achievement.

One of history's greatest books, Man's Search for Meaning, was not written by a king, president, or top CEO. It was written by a Jewish prisoner, who spent three years in the Nazi concentration camps. Viktor Frankl beat the 1:29 odds of survival and had this to say about it:

> Man is ultimately self-determining. What he becomes—within reason of endowment and environment—he has made out of himself. In the concentration camps, for example, in this living laboratory and this testing ground, we watched and witnessed some of our comrades behave like swine while others behaved like saints. Man has both potentialities within himself; which one is actualized depends on decisions but not on conditions.

Ultimately, the greatest prosperity and Bottom Line Results come from attitude, choices, and striving for balance over a spectrum of traits. It starts with a healthy purpose-driven mindset, thoughtfulness to the people in our lives, as well as attention to our growth and productivity. Optimal success comes from a conscientious plan to navigate through life and business utilizing the Bottom Line traits, and always staying clear of the Left Line and Right Line behaviors. Then, we must always incorporate the lessons—both good and bad—back where it all begins . . . a purpose-driven philosophical mindset.

Consequential Lessons

- There are great lessons in both triumphs and tragedies.
- We all make mistakes, and we all have successes. Share the lessons with others, and keep a journal.
- For every triumph, take a moment to have a celebration!
- When dealt a setback, modify the plans as possible.
- Even in the greatest problems, there is often a lot to be grateful for if you just pause and look.
- With some problems, the best strategy is to just sit back and wait it out. Time *does* heal all wounds.
- Even when the battle is lost, our efforts can inspire others.
- No leader is above making a poor decision.
- Everyone at every level is in the "business" of problem solving.
- Those who make plans and solve problems more effectively will excel over those who do not.
- People, businesses, and organizations remain viable only if they meet the needs and solve the problems of themselves, clients, members, or customers.
- Problems provide lessons; lessons provide value; value produces success.

Appendix A

Business Strategic Plan Outline

A "strategic plan" is actually more comprehensive than a "business plan," as it includes all of the information required for the management of a company, whether or not it is shared with outside parties. On the other hand, a business plan typically includes only the information that is shared with outside investors or bankers.

The following is an outline for a complete strategic plan, from which a business plan, policies and procedure manuals, and other documents may be derived. This outline is effective with both start-up and established operations, and may be modified to suit a particular business, as long as each area is addressed in one way or another.

1.0 Philosophical—*Get the "Big Picture"*
    1.1 Mission Statement
        1.1.1 Passion & Driving Forces
        1.1.2 Corporate Culture
    1.2 Executive Summary
2.0 Intellectual—*Do the Homework*
    2.1 Business Concept & Research
        2.1.1 Products & Services
        2.1.2 Technology
        2.1.3 Potential Uses
    2.2 Intellectual Property
        2.2.1 Trademarks
        2.2.2 Patents
        2.2.3 Copyrights
        2.2.4 Logos and Branding
    2.3 Training & Development
        2.3.1 Management Training
        2.3.2 Employee Training
3.0 Sociological—*Think 'Team Sport'*
    3.1 Corporate Structure
    3.2 Personnel
        3.2.1 Executive Team
        3.2.2 Key Employees
    3.3 Policies & Procedures

3.4   Employee & Management Review

3.5   Employee Recognition

3.6   Strategic Relationships

     3.6.1   Accounting

     3.6.2   Legal

     3.6.3   Insurance

     3.6.4   Bankers

     3.6.5   Suppliers & Vendors

3.7   Strategic Partners

3.8   Industry Associations

3.9   Government Regulators

3.10   Competitive Analysis

     3.10.1   Competitors

     3.10.2   Barriers to the Competition

4.0   Influential—*Get the Word Out*

4.1   Target Market

     4.1.1   Market Studies

     4.1.2   Customer or Client Surveys

         4.1.2.1   Primary Buyers

         4.1.2.2   Secondary Buyers

     4.1.3   Demographics

4.2   Marketing & Advertising

     4.2.1   Brochures & Catalogs

     4.2.2   Conventions

     4.2.3   Paid Media Advertising

     4.2.4   Database Marketing

     4.2.5   Assessment of Marketing Effectiveness

4.3   Public Relations and "Free" Media

     4.3.1   Newspapers

     4.3.2   Broadcasts

     4.3.3   Articles

4.4   Website

     4.4.1   Domains

     4.4.2   Current Design

     4.4.3   Updates & Maintenance

5.0   Physical—*Keep in Shape*

5.1   Products & Services

     5.1.1   Descriptions

     5.1.2   Strengths

     5.1.3   Weaknesses

5.2   Warranties

8.4.2.3 Competition

8.4.2.4 Litigation

8.4.2.5 Loss of Key Personnel

8.4.2.6 Crime

8.4.2.7 Employee Fraud

9.0 Operational—*Make It Happen*

9.1 Systems & Operations

9.1.1 Research & Development

9.1.2 Products or Services

9.1.2.1 Manufacturing

9.1.2.2 Service

9.1.2.3 Quality Control

9.1.3 Marketing

9.1.4 Sales

9.1.5 Order Processing

9.1.6 Shipping & Distribution

9.1.7 Delivery & Installation

9.1.8 Inventory

9.1.9 Maintenance

9.1.10 Accounting

9.1.11 Management

9.2 Customer Service

9.3 Crisis Management

10.0 Consequential—*Leave a Legacy*

10.1 Awards and Recognition

10.2 In-House Library

10.3 Key Lessons To Date

10.3.1 Proof of Concept

10.3.2 Proof of Management

10.3.3 Proof of Expansion

10.4 Supporting Documents

10.4.1 Credit Reports

10.4.2 Lease Documents

10.4.3 Contracts

10.5 Year-End Reports

Appendix B

Life Plan—An Individual Strategic Plan Outline

Most individuals do not think of themselves in the framework of a formal strategic plan, but it can be interesting to review the same categories, but in a personal context. Note how the "Life Plan" version integrates completely with the "Organizational" strategic plan.

1.0   Philosophical—*Get the "Big Picture"*
      1.1   Core Values
      1.2   Ethics
      1.3   Emotions
      1.4   Beliefs & Attitudes
            1.2.1   Religion
            1.2.2   Philosophy
            1.2.3   Spirituality
            1.2.4   Politics
2.0   Intellectual—*Do the Homework*
      2.1   Formal Education
            2.1.1   High School
            2.1.2   Training & Development
            2.1.3   Vocational School
            2.1.4   College
      2.1   Informal Education & Research
            2.1.1   Books
            2.1.2   Newspapers & Magazines
            2.1.3   Internet
            2.1.4   Television
            2.1.5   Parental Instructions
            2.1.6   Lessons from Parents, Others
            2.1.7   Experience
3.0   Sociological—*Think "Team Sport"*
      3.1   Family
            3.1.1   Immediate Family
            3.1.2   Extended Family
      3.2   Friends & Colleagues
            3.2.1   Close Friends
            3.2.2   Extended Friends
            3.2.3   Neighbors
            3.2.4   Business Colleagues

9.1.3   Activities
        9.1.3.1 Dining
        9.1.3.2 Entertainment
        9.1.3.3 Work
        9.1.3.4 Chores
        9.1.3.5 Travel
        9.1.3.6 Shopping
        9.1.3.7 Events
        9.1.3.8 Reading & Education
        9.1.3.9 Sleep & Relaxation

9.2   Daily Calendar
9.3   Crisis Management

10.0   Consequential—*Leave a Legacy*
10.1   Journal
10.2   Personal Library
10.3   Awards & Recognition
10.4   Keepsakes
    10.4.1   Photos
    10.4.2   Videos
    10.4.3   Mementos
10.5   Will and Trusts

Strategy 360 Worksheet

		Individual Plan	Organizational Plan
PURPOSE	Philosophical		
	Intellectual		
PEOPLE	Sociological		
	Influential		
PRODUCTIVITY	Physical		
	Environmental		
	Financial		
PROGRESS	Developmental		
	Operational		
	Consequential		

Appendix D

Bell's 5 Laws of Strategy

First Law: To achieve anything, we must have a strategy.

Second Law: "Purpose" sends us in the direction we will go.

Third Law: "People" are the ultimate priority.

Fourth Law: "Productivity" creates value.

Fifth Law: "Progress" is achieved by pioneers and innovators.